SAINT ME?!

SAINT ME?!

A practical guide to building and living your
personal plan toward sainthood

SCOTT A. FROYEN

ISBN: 1548394408
ISBN 13: 9781548394400

Dedicated to the communion of saints in heaven and on earth.

ACKNOWLEDGMENTS

THIS BOOK WOULD never have been completed without the encouragement and support of my spouse, Melanie. Thank you as always, sweetheart! And obviously it would not have been possible without my parents, Len and Gail Froyen. They were the first ones to read and provide valuable feedback on the initial draft. Thank you, Mom and Dad, for giving me life and your love. And thank you to Melanie's parents, Martin and Linda Kay Stevenson, for giving her life and allowing me to spend mine with her.

Now, since this is my first book (and maybe my last), I want to thank everyone who has contributed to my life to date--my grandparents, sister, brother, children, grandchildren, son-in-law, brothers and sister-in-law, niece and nephews. To all my friends over the years, my coaches and teammates, teachers and classmates, bosses and colleagues, priests and nuns, thank you all for the life lessons along the way. I believe we can learn something valuable from every single person we meet in our lifetime. All of you have certainly made that true for me.

Thank you to Cheryl Smith for her editing patience with a first-time author--talk about a learning opportunity. Also, thanks to the CreateSpace design team for their guidance and assistance throughout the self-publishing process. And finally, my heartfelt thanks to each of you reading this for your interest and for placing your trust in me to guide, motivate, and inspire you to strive for sainthood.

PREFACE

A S YOU WILL read soon, an outline of this book was divinely inspired. I really have no other way to explain how it came to be. Although I've never written a book, the words came quickly which I found to be a sign that this work was headed in the right direction. As it neared completion, I thought it might be a good idea to summarize the book's purpose and key points right up front. Although in the beginning I questioned what I had to offer that would help others, I now am convinced that if readers follow the guidance provided they could actually build themselves a good case for eventual entry into heaven. It's sure not easy to stick with every day, but the days I do are special. They will be for you as well. So here is my overview of the purpose, promise, and key ideas in this book.

Purpose: To guide, motivate, and inspire people to strive to become saints.

Promise: The active reader will come away with a personal plan toward sainthood and a sustainable way to attain success. At the very least, readers will be more aware of their current level of saintliness and more likely to improve upon it going forward. Best case, they will find their God-inspired life mission and work toward its fulfillment.

Key ideas:

- There are a lot of problems in the world.
- We were handed a perfect world by God.

- All the problems were created by us.
- Since we created them, we are capable of solving them.
- They were created through sin.
- We can solve them by avoiding sin.
- We were all created to become saints, that is, to strive to live a life worthy of the reward of heaven and eternal life.
- We achieve that through faith and works.
- Of course, God's grace is the determining factor, but we can at least build ourselves a strong case.
- We all have unique abilities and a God-given mission to find and fulfill.
- We should carry out that mission in a holy way.
- The root cause of sin are the vices: the seven deadly sins. Avoiding these through the demonstration of their contrary virtues is the path of the right way.
- If we do the right things (activities in line with our mission) in the right way (the virtues), we have the best possibility of becoming saints.
- We're talking little "s" saint here, not canonized big "S" Saint.
- To achieve something important requires planning and sustained effort.
- This book will walk you through the process of developing your own personal plan to strive for sainthood.
- It will also give you an engaging game to track your progress and provide ongoing motivation.
- And if you need a little inspiration along your journey, that will be provided as well.
- By the way, striving to become a saint is the only way for you to become truly happy in this life.

Unfortunately, I realize the odds are very low that I will succeed in convincing large numbers of people to strive for sainthood. But then again, if only a few of you succeed, many more may be inspired to follow your lead. Over a few generations, who knows what might happen? A few well-positioned saints around the world could make all the difference. Maybe we could finally solve all the persistent man-made world problems after all.

I choose to believe that we can. I am working hard on myself as a start. It is easy for me to get into a funk and think that the problems are too big and our will is too small to succeed. But why exist at all then? What is the purpose of it all? We are all here on earth to make a positive difference in the lives of others. This book will walk you through the process of determining what you specifically should do and how you should go about doing it. It's up to us to reverse the current trending in the wrong direction.

At this point, here is what I believe. We only need a few people who are willing to take up the challenge, and I pray you are one of them. I have worked hard to provide you with a simple process to develop your individual plan toward sainthood. I also pledge to provide you with ongoing support through The Saint Builder Foundation, saintbuilder.com. Of course, the hard work is up to you. But it will be worth it in this life and in getting to the next. I wish you all Godspeed!

TABLE OF CONTENTS

PART 1

INTRODUCTION

1

INTRODUCTION

"WHO WANTS TO be a saint? Come on, hands up if you want to be a saint." Our church was hosting a speaker for the evening who posed this question to begin his talk. Roughly 50 people were in attendance, but just a few hands went up. No, not mine. My quick personal assessment was, "Me become a saint? Yeah, right!" Just as quickly, I judged those with their hands raised and thought, "Wow, the arrogance. Who do they think they are?" Now I'm no biblical expert, but I do recall the more famous lines like, "Judge not, lest you be judged." I had already judged myself as unworthy, so it was okay to judge them too, right?

Our speaker then said something I'd never heard before: Everyone who makes it to heaven is, by definition, a saint. Really? I thought. Now I was sorry I had judged those who obviously already knew this; one more strike against me. And he did ask, "who wants to," not "who thinks they will be." Question re-asked and all hands go up. Yes, mine too. The alternative still seems more likely, but why not try? But then seriously, do I stand a chance? I've always loved a challenge, but only if there is some possibility of success. Let's just say I walked away from that talk with a lot of questions and some serious doubts.

Chief among the questions: Who am I to think I can be a saint? What would it take? What changes would I need to make? How do I get started? Is heaven even for real? How about hell? What will my wife think? How about family and friends? Is it worth the effort? Personally, I just tried to forget the whole thing and move on with life. Having recently retired after 33 years in business, I was supposed to be having fun all day, every day. Thinking about what it would take to become a saint sounded anything but fun. I don't recall hearing the word "fun" used to describe the lives of any of the saints. More like their lives were full of hard work and struggle-- oh and horrible deaths. Fun?

My test for accepting any job or work assignment has always been, Is this work important to others, and will it be personally interesting and challenging? If the answers are yes to all three criteria, then I can find a way to make it fun. Striving to become a saint certainly produces a positive answer to all three, so there must be a way to make it fun. No matter how hard I tried not to think about it, the idea of striving for sainthood would not leave my mind.

I left the corporate world and my role as a business executive to explore ways that I could use all I'd learned to truly make a difference in the world. I did a lot of praying, reading, and thinking to help determine how I should spend my time. Doing the traditional retirement activities was never going to be my answer.

Soon after the "saint" talk I started spending an hour each week at church in a silent practice we call Adoration. Basically it's a way to spend some quiet time with Jesus. I went each time to ask the question, "What do you want me to do with the rest of my life?" The short story here is that my personal mission and an outline for this book became clear during a couple of those sessions. The mission, strive to become a saint and help others to do the same. My reaction, "Are you talking to me? I am no spiritual expert. I believe in You, go to church, and try to be a good person; but strive to become a saint? And helping others-- what credibility do I have? No training, and certainly no sterling track record of walking the talk."

God's retort, "Look, you keep asking what you should do and now I've told you. You have business expertise in solving problems. I'm asking you to help me solve the root cause of all the world's problems: sin. I know you can do this by helping others develop their own personal plan to strive for sainthood. And by the way, start with yourself."

Good points. Guess that goes without saying. Think about it: no sin, no problems. In the beginning there were no problems. We were given everything we needed to survive and thrive as a species. We created all of our problems. So what's the obvious solution? Simple, everyone stop sinning. What is sin? Let's just call it "doing wrong" for now, more to come. If you believe that wrong is relative, this would be a good time to stop reading. Who doesn't sin? God; everybody else is out of luck. But saints sin less. Actually, some of them sinned a great deal until they became aware of the error in their ways. Then they did extraordinary things.

Okay, I get it: Help people become saints; solve all the world's problems. How do I do that? Use your business background to help fix yourself, and provide a proven business approach for others to follow. Give them simple, specific steps. Guide them through those steps, and help provide ongoing motivation and inspiration to keep everyone on track. Got it, I'll do my best. I have a lot to learn, but I was never one to argue with the boss, especially not the one who is asking now.

You may wonder why the title *sAin't Me?!* I just kept thinking that becoming a saint just ain't me. Then I realized that by adding an "s" to ain't, the word becomes saint. I can work with that. Saint me? That ain't me! Or the reverse, Ain't me? Well, why not try? Yes, saint me! How else can we make this ever increasingly unsaintly world better? Gotta start somewhere, might as well give it a try. Let it begin with me, and hopefully you. I'm taking a leap of faith on this one.

The goal of this book is to give you a simple path forward if you decide to take the leap with me. This is a how-to book, a step-by-step guide to becoming what I call a little "s" saint. We are not reaching for capital "S" canonized Saint here, just your everyday, run-of-the-mill, earthly person doing the right things in the right way. I hope we all overachieve and get to big "S" Saint, but save your miracles and martyrdom for later.

Thank you for your interest so far. My hope is that we can work together to support each other, saving the world from the mess we've created. My goal is to provide you with simple steps that are easy to understand and implement. Taken together, they will set you on the right path. It will take you 5 weeks, 6 days a week, 30 days in all to develop your personal life plan to striving for sainthood. Don't worry, these won't be long work days, maybe 30 minutes per day at the most. Are you willing to invest 15 hours in the next 5 weeks for the opportunity to potentially gain eternal life? Check out the suggested timeline in the Saint Builder Sandbox section at the end of this book (referred to as "Sandbox" from here on). Why Sandbox? Although this is obviously a serious topic I'd like to make sure we have some fun along the way. What's more fun than the times we had in the sandbox as children? Additionally, maybe we should think of this world as our shared sandbox. As saints, we would all be playing nice in it together.

My promise with this book is that at a minimum, you will be more aware of your current level of saintliness and will significantly improve upon it going forward. My hope is that you will find and fulfill your Holy Spirit-inspired life mission, become a saint, and live an eternally happy life in heaven.

When people ask me now, "So, what are you doing in retirement?" I respond, "Oh not much, just saving the world." When they respond with a laugh and a, "Really, how are you going about doing that?" I just say, "One person at a time, starting with me." If you're with me, let's get started. If not, I hope we meet again some day.

2

OLD MAN RANT

I N CASE YOU are on the fence about whether to devote yourself to striving for sainthood, allow me to give you a little more background. It will help to clarify where I was at in my thinking prior to accepting this mission. It may help you do the same for yourself.

My retirement goal was to find something significant to do in the world, guided by the Holy Spirit. I read many books, did some volunteering, and am participating in the religious education of teenagers. I've always enjoyed writing and have written many short articles on topics of interest as they come to mind. In reviewing those articles, I noticed that most of them are about things that annoy me. I'm going to summarize those things, as I believe they are part of what motivated me to embark on this saint-building challenge. Please indulge my old-man rant. Or don't, and feel free to move on.

It goes something like this. I'm annoyed and fed up with this world! If only I could be a kid again; everything made so much sense then. The rules were simple: Be nice and respectful to everyone, work hard to be your best at whatever you chose to do, and play by the rules of right and wrong that are self-evident. You will then be rewarded commensurate with what you do and how you do it. And the good guys always win!

Now, it seems that nearly the opposite is viewed as the better route to worldly success. It's goes something like this: Respect those you agree with and ridicule the rest, work less but expect more, and the end justifies the means, so go ahead and break the rules that don't help you get what you want. Right and wrong are relative, perception is at least as important as reality, what you say and what you do can be vastly different and that's okay.

Everyone is an expert at everything; just ask them. I thought I knew a lot coming into the workforce out of college but was promptly informed otherwise. I accepted that assessment; observed and listened to my bosses, coworkers, and clients; and worked long hours to gain valuable experience. Now, you can't convince most of the newcomers that they don't already know everything. They certainly don't have a confidence problem. Of course, they don't know what they don't know. I've heard this condition referred to as unconscious incompetence or the arrogance of ignorance. It makes me sad, like watching someone who can't sing try out for that television singing competition. They are stunned when finally given an honest appraisal of their ability. But with honesty comes the opportunity and motivation to improve.

Obviously there are exceptions (many I hope). Maybe I've just become the grumpy old man in the neighborhood yelling at kids to "get off my lawn!" Or maybe I should just give up on the old ideal and go along with the more "advanced" culture. I mean, why should we have to be nice to everyone, work hard, and be on our best behavior all the time when we can get what we want with much less effort?

We have become content with letting people tell us what to believe, since it's so much easier than actually reviewing the facts and coming to our own conclusions. Who has time to do the research required to form our own opinions in these fast-paced times? Plus, we'd have to consider alternative points of view to get to the truth. I already know I'm right because someone told me so when they told me what to believe. Remember when we were taught how to think, not what to think? In fact, that was the main purpose of education, challenging us to think and come to our own conclusions based on facts, to question everything and search for truth.

Good and evil used to be easy to spot. Now it's hard to tell. Bad guys win way too often. They are experts at making you believe they are the good guys. Or many times I don't think they even know they are the bad guys. We certainly don't. Confusion reigns. Everything bad is good, and everything good is bad. Cats and dogs living together! "What happens in Vegas, stays in Vegas." Come and be bad, have a good time...What?!

Anyhow, I've come to the conclusion that I should either (a) stop letting so many things irritate me and just go along to get along, or (b) do something about it. I choose b. I think the only way out of the mess is getting back to the basics that I hope we all still learn as children. How about if we were all nice to each other, worked hard, and played by the rules . . . simple! If we can replicate this in enough people, what a pleasant world it would be.

Here's our first assignment. Just for fun, try to be nice to everyone you interact with today and every day. Smile and greet everyone. Use the person's name. Expect the best. You will be amazed at the results. People may wonder what the deal is with you, but they will appreciate your kindness. Just spread your happiness and joy, even if you have to fake it in the beginning. What's the saying, fake it until you make it? Of course you will encounter some who will make this difficult. Remember, patience is a virtue. Give yourself a niceness score at the end of every day. I use a 1-10 scale, 10 being the nicest you can be. I am currently averaging a 7. Interestingly, my annoyance level actually went up initially. I got annoyed that people weren't always nice back, but that's my problem. Don't expect the world to change too quickly. Just feel good that you are doing your part.

Okay, rant done. Thanks for listening.

3

My Story

WHO AM I to think I'm worthy of helping people become saints? Just someone who thinks he is being called and is enthusiastically answering that call. I remember reading somewhere that when there is unity between God's will and ours, there is sanctity (saintliness). I remember this since it was a formula $W+w=S$, and I like math. Quick reference check . . . yep, got it right. Saint Maximilian Kolbe said it. More my speed, the Blues Brothers famously said, "We're on a mission from God." I think the same is true here. Actually looking back, I think this is what I was supposed to be doing all along. Maybe I have, in some small ways. The only thing I really enjoyed about my career was striving to be my best at whatever I was asked to do and helping others to do the same. That sort of ties in with this saint-mission thing.

I am sharing my story with you for a couple reasons. First, it may help to answer any credibility questions you may have. That is, why should you trust me to lead you in developing your plan toward sainthood? What do I know and how did I learn it? Great questions since you are considering spending your valuable time with me in the next 30 days. Second, I hope that by reading my brief story, you will be thinking about your own. Knowing your own story is an important component in developing your plan.

I achieved my goal of retiring from corporate America by doing everything you are supposed to do. You know, go to school, get good (enough) grades, get a good job, get married, have kids, buy a house, cars, etc., climb the ladder of success, and someday retire into a life of leisure. Mission accomplished, apparently. Problem is, I felt quite unfulfilled despite all the achievements and "having it all" in the eyes of others.

The fact is, I have been unhappy most of my life. Not an on anti-depression-meds unhappy, just not enjoying life. I have had many moments of happiness, but most of them have been fleeting. Most people would consider me very successful. I'm fortunate to have a beautiful and intelligent spouse, parents who instilled strong values in me, talented children and grandchildren. We have all the stuff you could want, great friends, and health that enables me to still play competitive tennis and the drums in a rock cover band. I get along with most people and have the ability to excel at whatever I choose to do. I have many accomplishments, resulting in a resumé that keeps recruiters calling. But with all this, I've only been truly happy approximately 14 percent of my life so far. (More on that later, including an opportunity to calculate your own happiness score if you'd like.) How can that be?

I was at my happiest at age 19, when I met my spouse. I believe she is one of the best people on the planet, as she shares her joy with everyone she encounters. I'm pretty sure most of our friends put up with me because they like her. Unlike me, she is happy most of the time. She is a registered nurse and loves the work of caring for others, especially saving babies. She chose wisely from the beginning.

I became a Certified Public Accountant, mainly because it came fairly easily and becoming a tennis pro or rock drummer didn't seem like a feasible way to make a living. I was attending a university known for its production of CPAs, and most of my friends were in the program. I liked the challenge of striving to pass the certification test on the first try, something few did, and being a CPA would pay for the standard of living we desired. All great worldly reasons, right?

With the help and encouragement of many fine leaders, I had great success in the business world, quickly rising through the ranks and leading others at a young age. Probably my extreme competitive nature, more than anything else, kept me moving forward. For whatever reason, I've always strived to be the best I can be at whatever I choose to do.

Basically my job over the years in leading finance, operations, and sales teams was to provide increasingly greater levels of value to customers, thereby earning their loyalty. It seemed I was always given the projects no one else wanted because these areas needed significant change, something many people would rather avoid. The challenge of working with others to make things better for customers, and usually for the workforce as well, at least kept life interesting. Jobs without this challenge were mind-numbing and tiresome.

I was fortunate to be a part of numerous success stories over many years. Then, at some point, it seemed to become increasingly difficult to get things done. For some reason we started talking more and doing less, letting "what's in it for me" become a more important question than "what's best for the customer." In other words we were trying to do the least amount of work possible to get the biggest reward possible. Shaping perceptions of what was getting done became more important than actually producing results. Very strange to me, but look at the world around us. Want proof? Haven't politicians been talking about the same problems all your life? How are they doing in solving them? Do they really want them solved? What would they do if they did? Self-preservation is pervasive. Makes one wonder.

In working with other like-minded individuals in large organizations across the country, I found that we were all facing the same issues. It's not an individual company problem; it's a cultural issue. To me, the over-riding problem seems to be people's individual desire to merely survive, not to thrive. Most people have settled for mediocrity rather than striving for excellence. Why is that? They are not inspired by what they do. They are, therefore, unhappy and just putting in their time. They live for the weekend so they can do what they really enjoy or at least have a distrac-tion from the daily grind. Sad, and seeing this trend escalate was a large part of my unhappiness.

Making things better for both customers and coworkers involved identifying problems, establishing improvement goals, finding solu-tions, and rallying people to implement those solutions. Winning that game over and over again kept me going. Unfortunately, it became in-creasingly difficult to understand what constituted winning. I once had a boss who constantly asked, "Are we winning?" My standard answer became, "What's today's definition, boss?" to which he just shrugged and chuckled.

Thankfully my work over 33 years afforded me the opportunity to jump out of the rat race and contemplate what should come next. In my goodbye message to the organization, I told them I didn't know what was next other than it not being travel since I don't like to, or spending more time with family because they may not want to. I did ask for suggestions and got some really funny and interesting stuff back. Cruise ship drum-mer was my favorite. Consultant, personal coach, writer, and speaker were the most prevalent.

I got advice from others who had retired, and from several books. Basically I learned you should do what you love, your passion, what you would do even if you weren't getting paid for it, the thing that gets you up in the morning with anticipation. Oh, and learn to say no to everything else. That will lead to true happiness. Nothing new here and easier said than done. Let's see, tennis pro, rock drummer? Hockey coach? Sports psychologist? All interesting but maybe not in line with doing something truly significant to benefit others.

How about that consultant, personal coach, writer, speaker thing? Of all the responsibilities over my career, these were the most enjoyable. I also received consistently outstanding performance marks for them. But what topics could I be passionate about where I also have credibility? What do I have to say that people would care about? Seems a stretch.

So I thought about the times in my life where I was truly happy, so that I could determine what those times had in common. It boiled down to striving to achieve something important that was challenging and interesting. How about I try to become the best I can be at life and help others do that as well? That would certainly fit the important, interesting, and challenging criteria.

To me, being the best at life involves doing the right things in the right way. It involves using your talents to help others in some way. Imagine what the world would be like if everyone was doing what they enjoyed doing, using their unique talents to the best of their ability for the benefit of others. We would likely be helping each other as our missions are probably intertwined. Everyone would be happy and helping each other. Maybe that's what our Creator had in mind in the first place.

Spoiler alert: Do not read any further if you believe this life is all we've got. You will never be able to do what I propose. Your motivation will waver over time and eventually fall off. You will find that the steps to striving for sainthood are easy to understand but difficult to follow consistently. They go against the current culture so you are always swimming upstream. Without belief in a higher power and purpose, you will fail when the going gets tough. Try if you want, but I've warned you. The promise of eternal life will sustain you, but only if you have belief and faith.

Ultimately the only way to fix the world is for each of us to fix ourselves first. This reminds me of a story I've heard many times about a child attempting to put together a puzzle, which was actually a torn-up magazine page. On one side was a photo of the world, on the other a picture of a man. The child put together the man and thereby the world on the other side. He told his father he fixed the man to fix the world. Great analogy!

Therefore, my mission of striving to become a saint, and helping others to do the same, is actually a mission of saving the world one person at a time, starting with me. Seriously, I truly believe the world was supposed to be what we think of as heaven: a beautiful place where we all get along and help each other to become the best we can be, given our unique skills and abilities. None of us can do it alone. I really think we were handed heaven and are slowly turning it into hell.

So I'm aiming high personally with a goal of becoming a saint. Sounds funny and out of reach, I know, but why not try? We only have one shot at it. And you can't become a saint without a true focus on others, so hopefully what I'm doing will help you too. I'll share my plan and learning to date, in hopes that it might inspire you to join me in the pursuit of sainthood. If we can populate the earth with aspiring saints, maybe we still have hope of reviving heaven on earth as it was originally meant to be. Now that would make me happy! How about you?

This book is about what I am doing personally. I think it can work for everyone. I'm learning as I go. I am no expert, but I do have a lot of relevant life experience. What a great teacher the past has been. I have no doubt that spiritual experts will take issue with some of this writing, and I welcome their input. I don't know what I don't know, so please feel free to educate me. I'll beg your indulgence for now. I've found that begging forgiveness moves things forward faster than asking for permission, something I would never have said before experiencing real life.

My goal is to give you a simple plan to follow. No matter where you are on your personal journey toward sainthood, you will find help. Many books have been written about why you should strive to become a saint so I won't spend time on that. Some talk about what you should do, so I'll spend a little more time on that. I have yet to find one that gives specific how- to steps, so this will be my main focus. Of course, making it happen is completely up to you.

My guarantee to you is simply this: If you take the time to develop your personal plan toward sainthood, you will be happier and so will all those with whom you interact. If you take it a step further and consistently act upon that plan, you have a real shot at gaining eternal life. It's obviously up to God's grace in the end, but what do you have to lose? Even if you just pick up one new saintly habit from the many discussed, you will significantly benefit yourself and others. I promise.

4

RELIGION AND POLITICS

Don't ever discuss religion or politics! Why not? You might offend someone. Really? But don't we come to a better understanding of truth when we debate things? I'm open to hearing and considering other viewpoints. Shouldn't we all be? Anyway, that's my opinion, and I'm going to share my thoughts on these topics briefly so you know where I am coming from. This may clarify thoughts to come and help you determine if you want to read further. Before beginning, please know that I have no expertise in either religion or politics. I merely have an interest in both, which has led to informal study over my lifetime.

First, I am a God-and-country type of guy, meaning I believe there is one God who created all things, that eternal life in heaven is attainable by us all, and that we each have a God-given mission to carry out in our time on earth. I also believe the United States of America was established through divine providence, that God led the founding fathers of our country to the principles that produced the greatest and quickest advancements in human history, at least for the first 200 years of our history.

More about religion for full disclosure. I am a practicing "cradle" Catholic Christian. That means I was born into a Catholic family and raised accordingly. In fact, my father is a deacon, or as my mother rightly says, they are a deacon couple. I do believe that the Catholic faith is the one handed down to us from Jesus and that the Apostle Peter was the first Pope. But I also understand the issues many have with the church and its leadership over its long history, and likely share some of their concerns. In my mind those issues are with the institution and not the faith. I believe all religions have more in common than they have differences. I am writing this for all but will confine myself to what I know.

With regard to politics, I have no party affiliation. I believe that all people were created equal and have the right to life, liberty, and the pursuit of happiness. I also believe that our common definition of these three terms have evolved over time. These are my personal definitions: life for all from conception to natural death, liberty for all as long as you are not infringing on someone else's liberty, and the pursuit of happiness through focus on your mission and helping others with theirs.

Now back to God. I believe that He created each of us with unique skills and abilities, implanted in us a specific mission, and gave us the innate ability to know right from wrong. Then to make things entertaining, he gave us free will. If we all discover and pursue our mission and refrain from sin, we would have heaven on earth. Unfortunately, it is rare to find many who are doing both, maybe just the Saints that have been officially recognized and now populate heaven above.

Think about it, without sin all the things we universally say we want--peace, food and clean water for all, a clean environment, equal rights and opportunity, etc.--would be a reality. Obviously they are not, even though our politicians constantly talk about these issues. Pick a side, it doesn't matter; no so-called solutions are working. None of them get to the heart of the matter, sin.

Only we the people, acting individually and together, can solve these problems by avoiding sin. Unfortunately, too many of us have been led to believe that the government is the answer. And we've been so successfully divided that we just argue. In Abraham Lincoln's words, "A house divided against itself cannot stand." And have you ever noticed that what politicians say often differs vastly from what they do, and the results are never as advertised? And on we go. . .

The only solution I see to getting us out of the mess we've created is to pursue sainthood. To me, we do that by doing the right things in the right way. The right things are those that are in line with our mission, and the right way is by being morally virtuous. Done together, this is the true pursuit of happiness. There is no other way.

To summarize, I believe in God and the possibility of eternal life; you don't have to, but it helps. I have a mission to pursue and so do you. You leave me alone to do my thing, and I'll do the same for you. If we can help each other, great. If not, I'm still rooting for your success. I won't do anything illegal or immoral and will hold you to that same standard. I am responsible for my results, and you are responsible for yours. But if you fail when putting in your best effort, I'm happy to help and trust you will do the same for me. And we should always help those who simply can't help themselves. Make sense?

I'm happy to listen if you can improve upon my thoughts above. I've actually developed a personal life philosophy that has my last name as its acronym. (See the Sandbox at the end of this book. I've also included a non-Froyen version for your use if it helps.) I do encourage you to take the time to develop your own. It will help you stay grounded in your beliefs when they are challenged. It's easy to become confused in a world that wants us that way.

5

QUICK START GUIDE

I F YOU ARE still with me, you must be serious, so let's get started. How about a "quick start guide," something you can do immediately? Seems that everything I buy now comes with a guide like this. I never bother to go any further unless absolutely necessary. So, if like me you have a short attention span, maybe this is all you will need for a while. It will help, but I do hope you continue.

Probably best to begin with a Bible verse. What's your first thought? John 3:16, right? Excellent choice, but I'm going with Matthew 22:37-39. **"You shall love the Lord, your God, with all your heart, with all your soul, and with all your mind. This is the greatest and the first commandment. The second is like it: You shall love your neighbor as yourself."** There's your quick start: Love God and your neighbors.

To show our love of God, how about we start and end every day with prayer? There are many formulas for prayer; do an internet search and pick one. The first one that came up in my search was ACTS. Taken from the book *Christian Prayer for Dummies*, It stands for Adoration, Confession, Thanksgiving, and Supplication. Self-explanatory for now, this is a quick start, with more to come later. Do this first thing when you wake up.

At the end of every day, do a review prayer. Ask, "What did I do well, what are opportunities for improvement, and what should I do tomorrow?" Then quietly and openly listen. By "openly," I mean, get yourself out of the way. You are listening to God. Try not to interrupt with your own opinion. If He wanted your opinion, He'd ask for it.☺

For extra credit throughout the day, say a quick prayer every time you have a choice to make. Our lives are the sum total of our choices. Therefore, it seems prudent to ask for God's advice at moments of choice. Some of them will actually be moments of truth, those big decisions that shape our lives. Simply ask for guidance, "God, what would you like me to do?" Then sit quietly and listen. Your answer may come immediately or it may take time, but it will come.

To show your love for neighbors, how about we just be nice to everyone we encounter each day? Since this was recommended earlier, you may have quick-started the quick start. Smile, say hello, and call them by name if you know it. If you don't and it's someone you see often, stop and introduce yourself. You would be surprised what an impact these simple things will make in the lives of others. I was. When I left the workforce, I had many people stop by my office to wish me well. Many said the same thing: They appreciated that I always greeted them by name and smiled. I thought that was just common courtesy, but they told me differently. Have you been scoring your niceness daily? How are you doing? I'm still at 7.

Action Items –

- Pray twice daily, first and last thing.
- Be nice to everyone, all day every day.

PART 2

STRATEGY

6

BUSINESS APPROACH

THE BALANCE OF this book is designed to guide you through the creation and implementation of your individual plans to strive for sainthood. A brief disclaimer first. As previously mentioned, I don't pretend to be an expert on what it takes to become a saint. But since God is the only real expert and I believe He is guiding this work, I'm going to carry on. Ultimately whether we make it into the club is up to His grace anyway. I'm simply a CPA with 33 years of business leadership experience. My focus was always on leading individuals and teams to achieve worthy goals and strive to reach their full potential. That is what I'm trying to do here. I'm writing using the knowledge I have accumulated over the years on the job and through formal education, training and self-study. I've been experimenting on myself, and I know what is working for me. That is what I am pleased to share with you.

Given my background, I'm recommending a business approach to striving to become a saint. What does that mean? Business to me is simply solving problems. The approach is basically to identify something that people need or want, a problem as they see it, and to find a solution. Then sell the solution, continually improve upon it, and find other problems and solutions. It's that simple.

Every successful business requires a plan. No plan, no progress. As Benjamin Franklin said, "If you fail to plan, you are planning to fail." No matter what you do, you are really in business for yourself. You are the solution to someone's problem. That's how we all earn a living. Even if you are a student at this point, you are getting paid to solve a problem. You are being supported today in order to solve a future need, even if it's only your parent's need to get you out of the house.☺

In this particular business approach, we will each develop an individual plan over the next 30 days. We have a problem to solve for the world and ourselves. There are not enough saints, and we need a plan to create more. Actually, we are going to develop two plans: (a) a strategic plan common to all of us aspiring saints and (b) an operational or tactical plan, as some refer to it, for each of us individually. Here are the basic components of the overall plan, followed by Figure 6a an image visualizing the overall plan:

1. Vision—the ideal state of existence in the future
2. Purpose—the main thing to strive for to achieve the vision
3. Objectives—high-level goals designed to achieve the purpose
4. Strategies—major areas of focus to achieve the objectives
5. Mission—your God-given individual reason for being
6. Goals—desired results designed to achieve the mission
7. Plans—detailed activities designed to achieve the goals

Figure 6a

Reading from the top down, each is meant to be a driver of the next level down. From the bottom up, each should support the level above. We will build this plan together. I have already developed our shared strategic plan, which you will read about in the next two chapters. If you agree, that takes care of sections 1-4. The operational plan, sections 5-7, will be completed by each of us individually, using a common framework. Basically, our plans will be answering two big questions:

1. What is our desired future?
2. How do we best move from our current reality to our desired future?

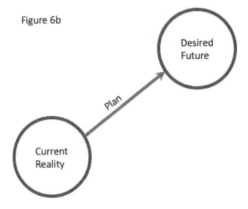

Figure 6b

The next steps after plan development are (a) an ongoing review and adjustment process and (b) a secret weapon to battle the demons. Yes, we will be battling demons, up to and including ourselves.

Are you ready? Next, I'll describe each step in some detail, provide my example, and give you the opportunity to develop your plan as we go. You may also develop your plan after reading the entire book. But I should note that the steps build upon one another, so I don't advise skipping steps. Even if you just give each section a cursory review and think about the work involved, that's better than skipping around. The forms in the Sandbox are essentially your personal-retreat workbook. I would flip back to that section now to get a feel for the work involved, and then decide which approach to take. I still recommend completing your plan as you read over the next 30 days. You can also find all the forms and my completed example at saintbuilder.com.

Although there is obviously work involved, my desire is always to make things as simple, specific, and streamlined as possible. I will give you my example and experience--the good, the bad, and the ugly--when absolutely necessary to ease your burden. And later, we will even make it fun through a game designed to track your progress.

7

THE MEANING OF LIFE

A S I STARTED writing this book, it dawned on me that if everyone were striving for sainthood, there would be a revival of heaven on earth. What do I mean by that? My recollection of the book of Genesis is that God created everything in six days and then rested on the seventh. Shortly thereafter, Adam and Eve screwed everything up. Let's review. God creates the universe and everything in it. He completes his creation with a man and a woman. He puts them in charge of everything with one simple rule: Don't eat an apple from one specific tree. Basically he gave them heaven on earth as long as they could refrain from breaking one commandment. Of course they break it, creating original sin and the rest is history.

Ever since, we've been chasing the happiness that must have existed in the beginning: no want for anything, peace and harmony, and beauty all around. There were no problems, can you imagine? The situation today is much different. Our sinful nature has produced a vicious cycle of ups and downs, rises and falls, ever since the apple incident. When you cut through it all, the ups took place when we were virtuous, and the downs were the result of sin. Very simple to understand really; so why do we insist on sinning and creating the falls on a seemingly endless basis?

Had there been no original sin, earth would still be heaven today, right? I don't know, but it seems to me like they had it all and threw it away. This was the first rags-to-riches story, in reverse.

One of my favorite quotes is from Albert Einstein: "The significant problems we have cannot be solved at the same level of thinking with which we created them." When I used this in a business context, I usually got blank looks followed by arguments about who created the problems. We waste too much time playing the blame game, rather than actually solving the problems. Can we please just stipulate that the cause of all our major problems is sin and that we are all to blame? If we can do this, we can resolve to actually fix them by limiting our sin and working peacefully together.

Personally, I think God was just trying to amuse himself by giving us free will. It may all just be a grand experiment He designed to see what would happen. He put us here, gave us all unique abilities and a mission that would produce heaven on earth. He then let us make our own choices to see what would happen. He is of course rooting for our success.

I think He hopes someday we will figure it out. The simple solution to restoring heaven on earth is for us all to strive for sainthood during our earthly lifetime. At some point the experiment must end. Based on the current state of things and the fact that falls are significantly outnumbering rises, it seems that ultimately we will destroy His first creation. Does He then simply recreate it and populate it with the few who did live as saints? Of course none of us knows, but I'd like to see whatever the new creation is. How about you?

My personal conclusion is that the meaning of life is to revive heaven on earth, as He meant it to be. Only through each of us individually striving to become saints can we make progress in that direction. Together, we can begin to re-establish heaven on earth and to populate the heaven above at an increasing pace.

If you agree, we have our shared vision of the future: Revive heaven on earth. A vision should be inspiring and easy to understand. Does this work for you? It does for me. Feel free to revise and expand upon it to make it yours. Then write it down and put it somewhere where you will see it every day.

SUMMARY -

- Vision: Revive heaven on earth

ACTION ITEMS -

- Write the above vision on a notecard.
- Add a further description of what it means to you and why achieving it will inspire you to action.
- Sign and date it to signal your commitment to working toward its achievement.
- Keep it somewhere where you will see and read it every single day.
- Optional: To be bold, share it with someone else. Maybe they will join you on your journey toward sainthood or at least remind you of your commitment along the way.

8

OUR PURPOSE IN LIFE

I F THE MEANING of life for us collectively is to revive heaven on earth, then the purpose of life for us individually is to become saints. At least that is a logical conclusion if you believe that God exists and that He implanted a moral compass, an innate set of skills and abilities, and instilled a specific mission in us all. If you believe these things, then read on. I won't be offended (saddened perhaps) if you don't. Anyway, it follows then that our purpose in life is to make the best use of our talents in order to find and fulfill our mission in a moral way. I think of this as doing the right things, in the right way. If we do this consistently, we at least have a chance of becoming saints. Let's just state here for the record that only through God's grace can anyone truly become a saint.

I had an old song running through my head, which I hadn't heard in years. It wouldn't go away so I figured in must mean something important. It was just the chorus over and over again: "ABC, it's easy as 1-2-3," etc. (Guess the artist and year.) In the meantime, what relevance does that song have here? Well, how about this?

The greatest commandment is found in Matthew 22:37-39. "You shall love the Lord, your God, with all your heart, with all your soul, and with all your mind. This is the greatest and the first commandment. The second is like it: You shall love your neighbor as yourself." (I realize this quote appeared in Chapter 5, but it bears repeating here, as you will see.) I remember reading somewhere that there are 40 words in this command-ment. The number 40 appears to have special significance such as 40 days and 40 nights in the great flood of Noah's time, and 40 days and nights that Jesus is tempted by the devil in the desert. There are other numbers that appear repeatedly in the Bible too like 3, 7, 33 and 144. So what? In don't know. I like numbers.

To comply with these greatest commandments, I believe we need to do at least the following, the ABC's and 1-2-3's:

To love God is to (A) believe in Him and express our gratitude for, well, everything, (B) seek and find the mission He gave us, and (C) do the best we can to fulfill that mission in a holy way.

To love neighbors (that's everyone else, by the way) is to (1) apply the Golden Rule – **"So whatever you wish that men would do to you, so do to them."**--Matthew 7:12, (2) help them seek and find their mission, and (3) support them in fulfilling their mission through our mission. ·

As the old song says, "ABC, easy as 1-2-3, simple as do re mi, ABC, 1-2-3, baby, you and me" (ABC, The Jackson 5, 1970). It takes us all work-ing together to be successful individually, and ultimately collectively, in order to make the world the place God intended it to be before Adam and Eve messed it up. So let's restore a heavenly earth by all doing what we were meant to do, helping others to do the same, and doing so in a holy way. By "holy," I mean virtuous (more on that in some depth later).

Another ABC, 1-2-3 just hit me. How about ABC, Actually Be Christian in serving 1-2-3, Jesus, Others, and You, in that order. I recently heard that you get JOY from observing this 1-2-3. Get it? You know, the ac-ronym JOY, Jesus, Others, You. Now I have the joy, joy, joy song in my head, and way down in my heart.

It dawns on me that throughout our lives we are juggling our attention between these JOY audiences. Now I'm reminded of a guy I once saw juggling while he ran a marathon. People who do this call themselves "jogglers." Getting back to joy and our marathon of life, I think maybe we should start a "joyglers" craze. Not sure how that works other than having three balls labeled Jesus, Others, and You. Anyway, the best way to learn to juggle is to start with one, quickly add the second, and then eventually the third. Start with Jesus, add Others, and then finally toss in You. Yes, I can juggle. It's a required capability for an aspiring tennis pro. You can too. Try it. I'll teach you later if you need help.

So there you have it. Our purpose in life is to strive to become saints. Follow the ABC's and 1-2-3's to get there. The easy way to remember this is by thinking, "right things, right way." And since I like math, I turned it into a formula to make it even easier: RT x RW x G = S. Translation: Do the right things (RT), in the right way (RW), and through the grace (G) of God be allowed into heaven as a saint (S). Notice the multiplication. If any element in the formula is a zero, we're out of luck. But actually that's not true, since the "G" is all that is really needed. Whatever--I'm sticking with it. If you prefer images to formulas, checkout Figures 8a below. The intersection of the RT and RW is where sainthood is possible. Faith in God and his grace will push them together, increasing your ability to live a holy life. By the way, the balance of this book is primarily designed to help you determine what the right things and right way are for you.

Figure 8a

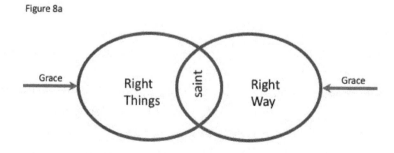

I hereby renew my personal pledge to strive for sainthood and to help you do the same. Although we can never be sure what our mission is in this life, I believe this is mine. I'm feeling truly hopeful and inspired for the first time in a long time. I'm certainly no saint at this point and feel a little embarrassed to believe that it's even possible. But what's the downside? That I become a better person? I hope you will join me. The fun part is about to begin.

Good news: We have completed our shared strategy, assuming you agree of course. I like it. Time to move on to develop your own individualized saint-striving plan.

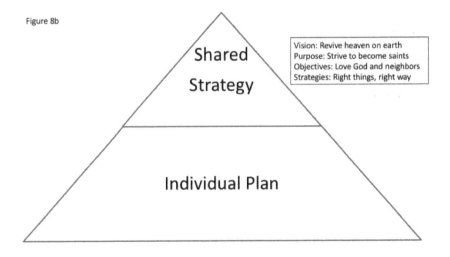

Figure 8b

Shared Strategy

Vision: Revive heaven on earth
Purpose: Strive to become saints
Objectives: Love God and neighbors
Strategies: Right things, right way

Individual Plan

SUMMARY -

- Purpose: Strive to become saints.
- Objectives: Love God and neighbors.
- Strategies: Do the right things in the right way.

ACTION ITEMS –

- Use the flipside of the Vision notecard from the last chapter to write down the above summary.
- Feel free to add a further description if helpful.
- Sign and date it to signal your commitment.
- Keep it somewhere where you will see and read it every single day.
- Optional: Share it with someone else if you dare. Maybe they will join you, or at least remind you of your commitment along the way.

PART 3

MISSION

9

USER AGREEMENT

I 'VE WRITTEN A "terms and conditions of use agreement" for us. It started out as a joke, but many of the points seemed important to share so I've kept it. How many of these agreements do you think you have electronically signed in your lifetime?

Here's a typical statement in a user agreement. "This site and its components are offered for informational purposes only; this site shall not be responsible or liable for the accuracy, usefulness, or availability of any information transmitted or made available via the site, and shall not be responsible or liable for any error or omissions in that information." Commentary on the agreement typically states that "this type of provision will help protect you against liability in case a user relies on your information and it causes a problem."

The above is then usually followed by something like this: "By accessing and using this service, you accept and agree to be bound by the terms and provisions of this agreement. In addition, when using these particular services, you shall be subject to any posted guidelines or rules applicable to such services. Any participation in this service will constitute acceptance of this agreement. If you do not agree to abide by the above, please do not use this service."

Taken together, these statements say to me, "We the provider of service are not responsible for anything, while you the user are responsible for everything." Aren't we paying them? This same company will constantly tell you it truly values your business--as long as you don't cause any trouble by trying to hold it accountable for what it has sold you. I've seen this attitude grow during my career to the point where it's now prevalent. It's an indication that no one trusts anyone anymore.

How about we strike an agreement based on mutual trust? I will tell you what can expect from me, what is required from you, and the results you are likely to achieve. I'll even give you a guarantee, with no legal interference. (I mean no offense to any of you lawyers. Once I thought about joining your ranks.) Don't worry, you won't be asked to sign anything. Here goes.

I hereby pledge to provide you with simple, easy-to-follow, step-by-step instructions for developing your individualized plan toward sainthood. This plan is action oriented not passive. If you take the action, you will achieve your intended result. That result is a morally lived life, filled with purpose and accomplishment. I have attempted to make the process interesting and even fun. In the end you will have a completed plan for success. My promise to you is that if you follow through on that plan, you will be a holier and happier person, as will all those with whom you interact. By simply reading this, you will be more aware of your current level of saintliness and more likely to improve upon it going forward. My hope is that you find and fulfill your God-inspired life mission.

Now here are a few cautions for you. While the steps appear easy, completing them will be difficult. They will make you think, and you will have serious decisions to make about your desired future. In fact, this may be the most challenging thing you ever do. No one is making you do it; it's completely up to you. There is no due date. The term "deadline" is particularly relevant here. Death is your deadline, and only God knows when that will occur.

This process requires an investment of your time upfront and then significant effort to build new habits and maintain your commitment. You already have a busy life; how can you add this? Thankfully our plans will not really require us to add to our current responsibilities. Rather, we will be incorporating some new things, dropping others, and probably prioritizing the rest differently.

It is important to understand at the outset that we will be fighting ourselves and the culture. In this lifelong battle, you will be your own worst enemy. I'm guessing it gets easier over time, but I don't yet have the experience to guarantee that. Are you getting nervous? Please don't be. Nothing of value is ever achieved without a little hard work. And we are talking about the ultimate value proposition here: eternal life in heaven.

We all have a decision to make. Do you want to be a saint or an ain't? It's that simple. Sure, you can rely upon grace alone, but why take that chance? The decisions we make and don't make define us. It's always easier to decide to do nothing than to do something. We will be developing some new habits to replace some old ones, and old habits die hard. You will be tempted to live with the status quo. Deciding to strive for sainthood will require you to get out of your comfort zone. Take the risk to reap the reward. What do you have to lose?

A great friend once challenged me to try out to play drums in a rock cover band. I hadn't played in one for over forty years. He said, "Come on, Froyen, get out of your comfort zone and live a little." I answered a drummer-wanted ad that night, attended three separate tryouts, and somehow got the job. I was so nervous and uncomfortable, but he was absolutely right. I've been in bands ever since. Thanks, Dave! If I can challenge myself in that little thing, why not for this most important of endeavors? "Come on, get out of your comfort zone, and live a little eternal life!"

It's decision time. You either choose (a) make a plan, take action, stretch yourself, and improve your odds through your faith and good works; or (b) make no plan, live with the status quo, stay in your comfort zone, and take your chances in gaining eternal life by depending on grace alone. Check out the Saint or Ain't Exercise in the Sandbox to help with your decision making. I hope you go all in with Option a. Let's develop your plan and have faith that God will be there to help you along the way.

Finally, here's your no-risk guarantee. I will give you a full refund of whatever you paid for this book, for any reason, within one year of purchase if you feel I haven't provided you the value you expected. Just send me your thoughts on what I could have done better to help you succeed and your receipt of course.

Are you ready to start planning your future? Let's go!

10

Mission Finder

D O YOU REMEMBER our saint-building formula? RT (right things) x RW (right way) x G (grace) = S (sainthood). Let's start with the first right thing, finding and working to fulfill your God-given mission. There are many other right things common to us all, and they will be discussed later in some depth. For now, let's concentrate on finding your mission.

I believe the most difficult and elusive task in life is answering the question, What does God want me to do with my time on earth? Finding the answer and living it out is our primary responsibility. I just found mine. So, obviously I am the expert you've been looking for to help you find yours. Yeah, right! I will share my true expertise: how not to find it. I have also conducted a significant amount of research on the topic of mission identification, which can be boiled down to some very specific and simple steps. One of my God-given gifts is making the complex simple--probably because simple is what I need in order to understand.

First, it may help to create some working definitions. Many similar terms are thrown around that seemingly mean the same thing. Here are the definitions that I propose we use.

- Purpose: The object toward which one strives or for which one exists (We have defined our shared purpose as striving to become saints.)
- Mission: A special assignment given to you by God
- Calling: An inner urge or strong impulse, especially one believed to be divinely inspired
- Vocation (Catholic version): The state of life chosen relative to the church: married, single, religious, or ordained
- Vocation (secular version): A regular occupation or way of life, especially one for which a person is particularly suited or qualified
- Career: A chosen pursuit in a profession or occupation

The mission and calling definitions are similar and are consistent with the intent of this chapter and book. Secular vocation and career are also similar and should ideally be guided by your mission. Many of us choose a career prior to understanding our mission. If we're lucky, we may find that our career coincides with our mission. If not, we may be able to incorporate our mission into our career. And some may need to plan a way out of their current career in order to live out their mission. If you haven't yet chosen a career, this section will help you choose wisely from the beginning.

Here's my quick test for knowing you've found your God-given special assignment: Your mission (a) makes the best use of your natural talents, abilities, and gifts; (b) has a significant benefit for others; and (c) is self-fulfilling—it makes you feel good about what you are doing. I think the order here is very important. Many books written on this topic suggest you start by identifying the things you love to do. But since we are to first love God and then neighbors, shouldn't we focus on things that they would love for us to do? Some propose that you must love yourself in order to love others. I believe you will grow to love yourself through your focus on others. In other words, if you use your gifts for the benefit of others, you will find self-fulfillment. If that equates to loving what you do, I see that as an added bonus.

While the test for determining whether you have found your mission is simple, the process to get there is anything but. Need proof? A quick Amazon book search on "finding mission" and "finding purpose" returned 478 and 1,523 books, respectively. That's a total of 2,001 titles on this topic, now that's a space odyssey. Sorry, old guy movie reference. I've read several of these books, and they basically say the same things in different ways. No offense to any of the authors; they are all just trying to help, and maybe one will help you. But try what I propose below first; it may save you some time. The hardest part is actually taking the time necessary to think for yourself. You may have more urgent things to do, but nothing more important.

Almost from the moment we are born, our life circumstances and those around us are a powerful influence, often determining what we can and should do. Most of us are shaped by the expectations of others, not by God's. I'm pretty sure God's plan for us all is not, "go to school, get good grades, get a good job, get married, have kids, buy lots of stuff, work hard for 40 years or so, retire, and then do what you really enjoy . . . or play golf."

When are we given the time to understand the infinite possibilities that exist? We are put in figurative boxes early on. Johnny is good at math, so he should become x. Jane is a science whiz, so she should be y. When you get to college, the big question is, What's your major? I think most of us just pick one to have an answer, and that answer may seal our fate. Once you start digging into that major, it becomes your career. If you are lucky, it's in line with your mission. If not, you probably sense that, but you are already dug in too deep to feel you can get out. A friend of mine says, "If you find you are digging a hole to nowhere, stop digging!" Excellent advice, Steve. Wish I would have met you earlier.

I fell into the trap of letting others steer me. Most of the friends I made at school were in the CPA program, and they all seemed so excited about it. The program was one of the best in the country, and the material came easily to me. Sign me up. Fate sealed. Had I thought about mission at the time, I would have chosen differently. I would have become a teacher and a coach. But they made no money, and my whole family was in that profession. I wanted something different. I wonder what God wanted. Priest maybe? But what I wanted brought me here, so all is not lost . . . yet.

What would you say if someone asked you today, "What is your mission in life?" If you have an answer, write it down now. If not, join the other 99 percent of us. I have yet to get a clear answer from anyone I've asked, but you will have an answer soon. Best case you will discover your lifelong mission quickly. On the other end of the spectrum, you might have to explore and find your mission in the next year or so. Most likely, you will end up with a general idea that will eventually evolve into your mission. That has been my experience. Long ago, I knew my mission involved striving to be my best self and helping others to do the same. I attempted to do that in my career whenever possible, and those were the best of times. Now that mission has been redirected to striving to become a saint and helping others to do the same, and it's all I want to do. Appears I've finally found it.

Below is a three-phase approach to finding your mission. It could reveal itself in any of these phases. I suggest you go through all three, even if you think you have found it early on. Doing this will provide additional verification that you got it right. It will also help to solidify it in your mind and begin to build your confidence that you can carry it out successfully.

One last recommendation before we get started. Schedule three separate one-hour blocks of time for yourself in the upcoming week. Space those times out to happen at least every other day, say Tuesday,

Thursday, and Saturday. **Exciting news flash:** You may know your mission by this coming Saturday! Find a location that is quiet and free of distractions, such as a church. Your home can work if nobody else is there and you are disciplined enough to focus only on this work. All you will need for each phase is the corresponding worksheet from the Sandbox, a writing utensil, your brain, and your faith. You "youngsters" will be tempted to use an electronic device to capture your thoughts, but please use the old-fashioned paper-and-pen method. Studies actually show it works better for this kind of task. Just trust me on this point. You can fancy it up later.

Phase I

Use the Mission Finder - Phase I, worksheet to answer the proposed questions and guide your thinking. You have one hour for this; it may take less, but don't let it take more. One caveat: Be honest--only you will see the answers. I say this because we all lie to ourselves at times in order to feel better about our situation. Maybe you wouldn't, but I have. Most of the time I don't even think we know we are lying. If you believe it to be true, would you pass a lie detector test?

Let's start by attempting to identify your current mission in life. A typical mission statement answers three main questions: (1) What do you do? (2) Who do you do it for? and (3) What benefit do they get from it? This should be the activity that you spend the bulk of your time performing. Write your answers to the three questions. Use the first thoughts that come to mind, which are likely the truth--a great place to start. Evaluation and revision will come next, but for now we simply need a starting point. I thought about sharing a couple of examples here but have found that this exercise is most helpful with little direction provided. Go.

Next, answer the second set of questions on the worksheet. These are all easy, closed-end, yes/no questions. For each answer, especially the yes's, ask yourself why. A common interrogation technique is to continually ask why to any answer. No matter what the answer to the previous why, ask it again. It helps to get to the truth, probably because it is annoying. (Three-year-olds would be great interrogators.) Anyway, asking why five times is thought to be the magic number. Try it. Some of your yes answers may become no's. No's usually stay that way. Do your best to be honest. Picture yourself justifying your answers to God. That always works for me.

Did you answer yes to these mission-affirming questions? Even when asking yourself why multiple times? If so, congratulations! What you are doing is very likely your true God-given mission. I am truly happy for you! I'm also very interested to hear how you came to find it in the first place. Maybe you can help guide, motivate, and inspire the rest of us. Humor me though, and go through the rest of the phases with us anyway. I'd appreciate your input on their value to you. It may also help to strengthen your resolve in carrying out your mission.

If you have some no answers, don't worry. I'm guessing very few of us will have all true yes answers the first time around. Also, in exploring your answers, you may have revised your definition of your current mission or identified an alternative. If so, capture it on the worksheet for use in the next phase.

Finally, please read the next section prior to ending your time today. It will get your subconscious working prior to the next scheduled hour.

PHASE II

Find your quiet place, worksheet, and pen. Within the next hour do the following:

- Start in prayer by asking God for help in understanding the mission he has in mind for you. Ask Him to please share with you what He would like you to do for Him. Sit quietly and listen. Who knows? He might make this process easy for you and reveal it immediately. Remember those scripture readings "seek and you will find," "ask and it will be given," "knock and the door will be opened"? Give them a try. Write down everything that comes to mind.

- Now, think about your unique strengths, the things you are naturally good at. Draw from past experience and what others you trust have observed in you. You might even ask others prior to your quiet time, but rely more on yourself. Who knows you better? God for sure, and you can ask him too. Write down your strengths.

- Next, write about things you are interested in, the things you enjoy doing in your free time. Don't include all the entertainment-type activities you do purely for enjoyment, but meaningful activities that make life better for yourself and others. Or things you don't currently do but would like to do someday. Please don't dismiss anything that comes to mind. Judging them will come later.

- Review your lists of strengths and interests. Is there a clear mission in there somewhere? Ask God again to tell you what your mission is. Listen again. Sit in silence and listen. Think of nothing, just be at peace. Write down everything you hear with no judgment or analysis. When your thoughts run dry, stop.

- Now go back to the questions in Phase I. If you embarked on the mission you wrote down, would you be able to answer "yes" to all of them? If so, you may have it.

- If not, just walk away for now, knowing your subconscious will continue to work on this while you go on with your life. Let it lie until the last scheduled hour. Keep your pen and paper handy at all times, especially by your bedside. Immediately write down the random thoughts that come at you. You risk losing them if you don't.

- A revised or alternate potential mission may come to you in this process. If so, capture it on the bottom of the worksheet.

- Read through the Phase III section below in preparation for your next session.

PHASE III

Okay, last scheduled hour, time to go all out and finish this mission identification thing. Got a fancy business tool for your use. It's really just a simple four-box matrix called a SWOT, which stand for strengths, weaknesses, opportunities, and threats. You have already done some thinking on this in Phase II. Its purpose is to help evaluate the current state of a business from both an internal (strengths and weaknesses) and external (opportunities and threats) perspective. It is typically used to provide relevant background information to assist in developing future business plans. For us, it will help to answer some lingering questions.

The main internal-view questions are (a) What natural and acquired talents do we possess that should be built upon? and (b) What personal weaknesses do we have that must be overcome or at least acknowledged? The external-view questions are (a) What can we do to provide value to others? and (b) What are the barriers to our being successful in providing that value?

Here's a process to follow to complete the matrix:

- Think through these categories one at a time, and complete the four quadrants.
- Start with strengths. You should have a good list from Phase II. Review it and make any needed updates, making sure you are comfortable that they are a true and complete representation.
- For opportunities, start with the list you captured in the "Your Interests" section of Phase II.
- Ask the question a different way: What do people need or want that I can provide, given my natural and acquired talents? List as many as you can think of without judging them.
- Weaknesses and threats could actually be your hang-ups in getting to mission. No matter how hard we might try, some of us are always evaluating our ideas through a lens of negativity. We see the downside of everything too quickly. We are glass-half-empty

types. I've tried to minimize this negative side, but we might as well face the facts. There will be difficultly in carrying out any worthy mission. We all have some weaknesses, and external threats to our success are a reality of life. It is beneficial to recognize them upfront to be prepared when they do arise.

- List your weaknesses, or as I like to think of them, opportunities for improvement. We all have them. Be honest and list them all. I found it helpful to think about traits of others that I envy or am annoyed by. Some of them are weaknesses of mine. I realize that envy and annoyance are not saint-worthy. I listed them as weaknesses too.
- Look through your weakness list. Circle the ones you want to overcome or maybe even turn into strengths.
- Last, external threats, or barriers to success posed out in the world. These might be common to us all. One challenge is always getting over the "what others might think" barrier. Another one might be figuring out how you will make a living with your mission.
- Now go back to the opportunity section. Can you see a mission that matches your strengths and is compelling enough to motivate you to overcome your weaknesses and the threats you will face?
- A good test for knowing if you have identified a compelling mission is asking yourself if you would be willing to work on it on a Friday night or Saturday morning. Those are the times I really just want to zone out and do nothing. If I could substitute something for nothing in those times, what would it be?
- Write down any potential mission you identify.
- Now go back to the questions in Phase I once again. If you embarked on this mission, would you be able to answer yes to all of the questions?

Have you found your mission? Even if you only have a general idea, that's better than nothing. If not, don't worry, it will probably reveal itself to you as we continue. If we get to the end of the book and you still don't have your answer, maybe a book from one of the experts will help. But I do believe it will come to you. Keep writing down your random thoughts.

Here's another common problem, your mission may come to you and you may resist it. Maybe the weaknesses and threats seem overwhelming. Or you just don't want to get out of your comfort zone. Maybe it will require significant change and courage. Looking back, I knew my mission at least fifteen years ago, but I was in my comfort zone at my job, even though I didn't like it. Ask yourself honestly if this applies to you. If so, you have two choices: (a) Face your fears, get out of your comfort zone, commit to your mission, and get moving; or (b) continue to be trapped in the prison you have created for yourself. I really think it's that simple. It was for me. In the next chapter I'll show you how I finally got over it. If you don't have this problem, you can skip it. I hope you are one of the fortunate ones.

Last thing, please take the time to complete the worksheets in all three phases before moving on. I've read books that state something like this, and I rarely paid attention. I'd tell myself that I would go back later, but I never did. You may be more disciplined. I urge you to give yourself the time needed to think about what your true mission is before moving on. The rest will become much easier.

Please don't delay. The problem with this kind of work is that it has no deadline. For us procrastinators, this is a big problem. We thrive on deadlines, ignoring them until the last minute and then loving the adrenaline rush of getting the work done just in time. Please don't be like me. There is no time like the present. It's all we have. This could be a moment of truth for you. Right here, right now. Don't ignore it, do it now! You will be thankful you did, maybe for all of eternity.

11

HAPPINESS

I F YOU ARE stuck on the mission identification work of the previous chapter, I have one more step that may help. As mentioned numerous times, my mission came to me quite clearly long ago. At the time, I wasn't ready to believe or accept it. I went through the process laid out in the previous chapter and got the same answer. Still I wasn't ready to commit. But I was not content in status quo life, so I decided to explore in some depth why that was. Ultimately, the exercise described below motivated me to finally commit.

I decided to take a virtual tour of my life to date and chart my level of happiness throughout. By finding my happiest times and determining what created that happy state, I thought that maybe I could identify a mission that would serve to recreate more of those times. Since I'm a CPA and like charts, I put one on a blank sheet of paper where the horizontal axis represented the years of my life, and the vertical was a self-scored subjective happiness level from 1-10, 10 being happiest. I plotted the big life events first--graduations, marriage, children, jobs, etc.--then went back and gave every year a score. Finally, I did a bunch of math to determine what percentage of my life so far has been very happy (8-10), very unhappy (1-3), and everything else in between.

The results were 14, 7, and 79 percent, respectively. On the good-news front, I have been very happy twice as much as very unhappy; on the kind of sad side, only 14 percent very happy. That's about 8 years total, or about 2,900 days out of 21,000 total lived. (Guess my age.) More good news: Turning the 79 percent of okay times into very happy would result in a 93 percent happiness rate. I'd settle for 80 percent. I have 24 years left according to some random life expectancy table. If I can live them out at an 80 percent 8-10's on the happiness scale, that would add about 8,700 very happy days, for a total of 11,600 in a 29,600-day life, nearly 40%. Way better than 14% and ending on a high note.

Apparently I should have started this saint pursuit much earlier. If I had begun 15 years ago, it would have added 4,400 more very happy days, over 50% of my lifetime . . . oops. And the best news, if very happy turns into sainthood, an eternity of happiness awaits. What do I have to lose by trying? What am I waiting for? This became the motivation that finally got me to accept my mission and get moving. Try it for yourself. Complete the Happiness Index in the Sandbox.

Whoa, quick time out. I just looked at the number of words written in this section, 666 (of Book of Revelations fame); is that a bad sign? Actually I think the devil just wants to throw me off my game. Earlier in the week, when I was going to my office, I noticed a water mark in the ceiling. An hour later I had found the source of the problem and arranged for a repair. Then I sat down to write, and the house smoke alarms went off. No kidding. I just had to laugh and inform satan that since he had set them off a month earlier, I already knew how to deal with that quickly. Sure, it took me another hour, but it didn't throw me off as much as the first time, so ha! Okay, up to 800 words now, so crisis averted.

In analyzing the happiness chart and the things that led to the highs and lows, my discovery was that I am happiest when I am (a) learning something new, (b) striving to get better at something, (c) solving big problems, (d) achieving worthwhile goals, and (e) helping others to do the same. What I am best at is setting and achieving goals. What more important goal is there than striving to become a saint? Perfect fit, I'm in . . . finally!

Did the Happiness Index exercise help you determine what you should be doing to improve your personal happiness going forward? What has made you happy in the past and why? How can you do more of those things going forward? Answering these questions will likely work you right into your mission. It's simple, but likely not easy, since you still have to make a living. You may find that the way you earn your living today is not in line with your true mission. If that is the case, not to worry, you can develop a plan to get on mission over time. There may also be ways that you can incorporate mission-relevant activities into your current role. Regardless of where you are at in life and how closely you are living your mission today, you will have a plan to get or keep yourself on track soon.

Please allow me to state this one more time. I truly believe we were each placed on earth with a specific mission. If we were all clear on what that mission was and pursued it to the best of our ability, the world would be what God intended it to be: heaven. Of course we are not specifically told what that mission is, or maybe we just don't listen. And our freewill allows us to do as we please. For most of us, that ends up being what others expect of us. The way to know if you are on the right path is to ask yourself if you are happy most of the time. Like you can't wait to wake up every day and do what you do. Only when you have alignment with God's mission for you will you be truly happy.

PART 4

THE RIGHT THINGS

12

HABITS

O NE LAST THING before getting into more specific right things that apply to us all. My aim is to help us create a framework for our choices
and instill habits that will lead us toward sainthood. If you haven't noticed, I say "us," "our," and "we" frequently. I use these words because
we are all in this together. Without supporting each other, it would be
difficult for any of us to stay the course. Building a community of aspiring
saints will help us all to thrive. (More on that later.)

My objective is to provide specific, simple, easy-to-implement steps
that can be incorporated seamlessly into your already busy life. When
taken consistently, these steps will become habits. Repetition is key. Like
many things we do in life, once the steps become habits, they no longer
seem difficult. Getting into the habit and remaining devoted is the tricky
part. I've heard many times that it takes at least three weeks to instill a
new habit. Please commit yourself to at least that. I'm not sure how long
it takes to actually sustain a new habit. Let's find out together.

My personal goal is to ingrain these habits into my being, my muscle
memory. In this case the muscle is the brain. If we do something often

enough, over time we don't even have to think about it anymore; it just happens, like walking, riding a bike, or juggling. In fact, once we've attained this auto-pilot ability, thinking actually gets in the way. I once thought about riding my bike when I was going 40 mph downhill. It got scary and I nearly fell. No more bike thinking for me.

Think of your own examples to convince yourself this is true. It is important to understand that the new habits we will discuss may be difficult initially, but will become simple and powerful over time. This knowledge will help provide the motivation you will need in the beginning. Here are a couple of examples and a story. I have played tennis and the drums for over 40 years. When I adopt a just-go-out-and-enjoy attitude, all goes well and the results are positive. If, on the other hand, I get too serious and overthink what I'm doing, stress and a less than stellar performance ensue. My best performances have been when I give my effort up to God as a thank you for the abilities he's given me. Faith and trust lead to amazing accomplishments. Alternatively, if my aim is to demonstrate how good I am to others through my own hard work, a look-at-me attitude, failure is just around the corner. Strange but true.

One last quick story that brought this all home for me. I was once given the "opportunity" to present an award to a city for an accomplishment they had achieved. The scheduled presenter had a conflict, and "fortunately" I did not. I had virtually no background on the subject matter, yet was always considered a reliable speaker regardless of the topic. I got on a plane with a bunch of reading material and two hours to prepare. No problem. This was a small town of about ten thousand people. How big a deal could it really be? I spoke in front of groups all the time, so no sweat.

Little did I know that it was a big deal to them, and media coverage was going to be widespread. Upon arrival, I was introduced to all the town dignitaries who were very excited to share their news with whoever would listen, the entire state of Iowa hopefully. I saw the stage, TV cameras, and the crowd and went into a slight panic, maybe more than that. I'm an off-the-cuff-type speaker, no notes, just what's in my head. It was time to get serious. Oops, brain freeze, and not the delicious ice-cream type. All I could think to do was pray that the right words would come. I had the punch line down cold: "I'm proud to present xyz city with the first 1-2-3 award in the state."

Okay, a little calmer now. Faking an injury was out of the question, too late. I was introduced, walked up, surveyed the audience of maybe a couple hundred, and saw way too many cameras and microphones. It appeared they were expecting someone to say something interesting and important. I asked for guidance from up above one more time and started talking. Delivered a joke. Lots of laughter. Whew! I felt an inner calm and went into opening remarks. I could see that they were listening intently. Wow, amazing.

Then, out of nowhere came this thought. "You are amazing, no preparation, big moment, and you're hitting it out of the park." Big mistake . . . Pride! This happened just at the moment of punch-line delivery. And I froze, totally forgetting the only line I had practiced. I panicked inside, laughed at myself. Then smiled and cracked another joke. Thankfully more laughter and I delivered the line. Mission accomplished. Interviews for TV and radio followed, and all went well. Lesson learned: Trust in God, and all is good. Trust in yourself, yeah, good luck with that.

Back to habits. Hard work always precedes worthy accomplishments. Ingraining a habit is hard work, requiring study, practice, and self-discipline. We all have natural abilities that get us started. Pushing past what comes naturally in the pursuit of excellence is the challenge and fun in life. So our goal here is to learn the steps, practice them daily, and eventually just live them, trusting that they will move us in the right direction and lead to the intended result--sainthood!

Finally, I'm not trying to reinvent the wheel here. I will present what I have learned from my education, training, and wide range of life experiences. I do not claim to be a spiritual expert. Those of you who are might take issue with some of the things I say. I hope not, but I do know that I don't know what I don't know. Got that? The thing is, I feel compelled to get this information out as quickly as possible. Therefore, I'll just beg your forgiveness rather than ask for your permission at this time. I welcome your thoughts and suggestions for improvement and pledge to seriously consider them all going forward.

13

THE TIME OF MY LIFE

H OPEFULLY YOU NOW have a clear picture of your mission in life or at least know what your focus should be in the near term. Knowing your mission provides a framework for decision making for the rest of your life. It helps determine what you should and should not do. To understand what matters most and to avoid things that matter least. It helps you always live in the present, moving forward by doing the daily tasks that result in big achievements over time. Knowing your mission helps you do the right things.

The major difference between those who accomplish big things in life and those who do not is how they spend their time. We all have the same amount of time in a day, but why do some get so much more done than others? Those people know what they want to achieve and structure their activities accordingly. They spend their time wisely, not wasting it on meaningless activities. Spending time is like spending money: You can invest it wisely on activities that produce a future value or spend it on things that eventually become worthless.

Our grandchildren like to play board games. When they visit, we bring out the ones we played as kids. Remember The Game of Life? It has a cool roulette-type wheel attached right to the board. Spinning that wheel determines your fake-life fate. On a recent visit, our youngest grandchild, age 10, ended up with two sons and two daughters. He gave them all names beginning with "J," maybe because his family all have "L" letter names. His father remarked that he hoped the boys would be just like his son (their "father" in the game). This was one of those ambiguous comments, like the saying, "May you live in interesting times." It will be interesting to watch what happens to him in his real life. Thankfully, we determine our own fate through our choices, not through the roulette wheel.

Following their visit, I started tracking my time in the game of real life. I am always busy doing something and was curious about how much time I was actually investing versus spending. The first week was certainly eye-opening. Using a weekly calendar, I wrote in what I did during my waking hours. I then labeled the activities as either "V" for valuable or "W" for waste at the end of each day. I made the determination based on the usefulness of the activity toward achieving my mission. Admittedly a bit arbitrary and subjective, but it turned out to be a good little research project.

Any research usually reveals both good and bad news. For me, the bad news was that I was wasting a whole lot of time, 62 percent of my waking hours, to be exact. And that was probably a better-than-usual result, simply because I was paying attention. The good news is that I now had a baseline, a starting point to compare with future results. Investing more that 38 percent of my time on valuable activities going forward shouldn't be too difficult to accomplish. Just being aware of this dismal result should drive an immediate time allocation improvement.

"Squirrel!" I have a band friend who occasionally yells this and then launches into some song that just entered his head from out of nowhere. Well, here's a story that just came to me. Have you ever seen the fictional character Father Guido Sarducci, created by comedian Don Novello? He did a bit about paying for our sins, which went something like this. God greets you at the gates of heaven and pays you for your time on earth, like $10 a day. Then you have to pay Him for your sins. If you have anything left at the end, He lets you in. So my squirrel thought was, What if something similar happened with how we spent our time? I'm just guessing that wasting over half of it will be frowned upon.

I told a friend about my little experiment and its discouraging results. He had two observations: (a) What do you care--isn't that the way it's supposed to be in retirement? and (b) if it really bothers you, come back to work so you'll at least be productive ten to twelve hours a day. Well, it does bother me, but I'm not going back. Then I wondered if I was really that productive during those working years. If my mission during those years was to support a family and put me in a position to retire early and do this, then yes, I did what was expected to get paid. From a customer perspective, maybe, the 80/20 rule applied. That is, 20 percent of your efforts produce 80 percent of your results, so maybe really just a couple hours a day are productive? Of course, no one is ever going to admit to that while still employed. Never mind, ignore this for now.

Now it's your turn to develop a baseline. Use the simple "valuable" or "waste" labels initially. If you keep a weekly calendar, go through your most recent one applying a "V" or "W" to each activity. If you haven't been keeping a calendar, start. It truly will be one of your keys to success going forward. You don't need to buy a fancy planner. I use a calendar that lists the days of the week across the top (Monday through Saturday), and my waking hours of the day down the side (6 a.m. to 10 p.m. in my case). Draw your own on a page if that's easiest, or use fancy technology if that's what you like.

It is completely up to you to determine value based on your individual mission. You are on the honor system here. If you cheat, you are only hurting yourself and your chances of becoming a saint. That's what your parents would say, right?

Here are my suggestions for classifying something as valuable. If you are in school working on meeting graduation requirements, all class hours and study time are valuable. For you family managers (the term I found for stay-at-home moms and dads), the glue you use to hold it all together for everyone else is obviously valuable. And if you are employed or self-employed, anything you must do in order to get paid is valuable. And you might want to consider if there are ways you could allocate more time to things that truly matter to customers, things they would be happy to pay for if they knew about them. You might find that you can reallocate your time to increase your value to customers, which will in turn likely increase your value to your employer. Just a little free advice there--let me know when your raise comes through.

Keep track every day for a week. Add up the "V" hours and divide the result by your total waking hours. As an example, my first week valuable hours' total was 36. There are 24 hours in a day, minus 8 hours for sleep (for me anyway, use your own number). That leaves 16 waking hours a day. Multiply this by 6 days (remember to rest on Sunday), for a total of 96 hours. Dividing the 36 valuable hours by the 96 waking hours equals 37.5%, rounded up to 38% valuable use of time. For you glass-half-empties, that's 62% wasted time.

What's your baseline number? Are you happy with it? Does it surprise you? More time to think about this later. Let's move on.

SUMMARY –

- How you invest your time will determine your level of success in life.
- A valuable use of time is anything that helps you carry out your mission.
- All else is waste.

Action Items –

- If you use a weekly calendar to track your activities, use your most recent one.
- If not, start using one this week.
- Mark each daily activity for all your waking hours with either a "V" for valuable or a "W" for waste.
- The definition for valuable is anything that helps you carry out your mission.
- Add up your total "V" and "W" hours for the week, excluding Sunday.
- Divide your "V" hours by your total waking hours, that is, V/(V+W). This is your baseline percentage of time spent on valuable activities. One minus this percentage is your wasteful percentage of time for the week.
- Are you happy with the result? More to come, moving on.

14

PLAYTIME

P LAYTIME WAS MY best subject in kindergarten: the chance to go outside and run around. It's the only thing that got me through the rest of the blah, blah, blah. Recess should be incorporated into every workday. We want people to be healthy, so we build fancy gyms. How about just having a recess bell and let everyone go wild? Apparently, I almost got held back for rarely talking to the teacher back then. In a parent-teacher conference, I was asked why I didn't talk to the teacher, and I answered, "We don't really have anything in common." That's the way I remember it now anyway. It worked, so on to first grade!

So what does playtime have to do with striving for sainthood? Well, in tracking my time over many weeks using the "V" and "W" labels, I found that they fit into six general categories. The first letters of these categories form the acronym PLAYER. The first four, forming "PLAY," are the activities I was labeling as "V." We are all players in the real game of life; let's play it well. Maybe a little too cutesy, but since it happened by accident and we are supposed to be having some fun along the journey toward sainthood, I'm sticking with it.

These are general categories that apply to us all, and they also happen to fit the major areas identified by many experts in the leading-a-healthy-life field: physical, mental, emotional, and spiritual. Some experts also throw in a financial category. Many say you need to keep these areas of life in balance. I'm not sure what that means or if it is even possible, practical, or necessary. I've never understood the term work-life balance. Isn't work part of life? How do you balance something that's part of something else? I choose to think of them all as important and essential components of our lives that each need attention.

Squirrel! Philosophy was my minor in college for a time. Until one fateful day when the professor put an empty cup on the round table we sat at (It was a small class--go figure). We were asked to describe what we saw. I was going to be the last to speak, and I was hoping that some deep and profound thought would come to me as others spoke. Each of my classmates went into great detail, like ten minutes each, but no revelation came to me. Why pretend? "All I really see is an empty cup on the table." Looks of disbelief. I was an outcast. After class I asked the professor what he saw, and he said, "The same as you, but I'll deny I just said that." We laughed and agreed that philosophy wasn't really my thing. I got the feeling he wished it wasn't his either. My point is, don't make things harder than they need to be.

And the categories are **Pray**, **Learn**, **Act**, **Y**outhify, **E**verything else, and **R**est. Okay, so I made up "youthify" to get the "y." I had a whole grouping of valuable activities with a similar theme but no catchy name. Then I noticed that a "y" name would give me an acronym. It fits, as you will see soon enough. Please stick with me while I explain each. You can go out and play when we get done.

Pray--Start each day with prayer. Then ask for guidance throughout the day, whenever it seems appropriate. Somewhere in the Bible it says to pray always. I find that the more I do, the more I get done and the better I feel. It keeps me focused. I now set a phone alarm for every waking hour. I say a quick thank you for the last hour, and ask for guidance in the next--simple. Or I might just say a standard prayer if I have nothing specific to say. End the day in prayer as well.

Take two minutes to think about your current prayer life. What are you doing currently? What is working that you will continue to do? What things would you like to consider doing in the future? Use the Potential PLAY Activities form available in the Sandbox. Write as many possibilities as you can think of. Ignore your real-life time constraints for now. Later, I will provide some ideas for you to consider in developing your specific plan. For the time being, just capture your stream of consciousness.

Learn--Become a lifelong learner if you aren't already. Learn what? Anything you are interested in. Subjects that fascinate you. A skill you would like to learn. A place you want to go someday. Something you want to get better at. People you admire and would like to emulate, maybe the big-S Saints. How about this, research the facts and truth about frequently debated topics to determine your own stance. Just start with anything you feel compelled to know more about.

Of course the best situation is when what you are learning advances your mission. For instance, I am currently learning how to become a gooder, I mean better, writer. This is a direct tie to mission. I'm also learning a challenging drum rhythm and how to improve my pool and chess playing. Tie to mission? Getting better at something gives me confidence that I can do all things in Christ, who strengthens me. I think that's the right wording. No, I'm not going to look it up. For further justification, playing pool and chess both require that you think ahead a couple of moves, which helps with critical thinking and decision making. I am rereading the Bible as another example of learning. And soccer-ball dribbling techniques.

Take a moment and write a list of things you would like to learn. Write a long list; you can prioritize it later. In fact, I recommend you keep a running list. Use a little notebook that you can carry around to keep track of ideas and record your progress. I'll never get mine all done. It seems that learning creates a curiosity to learn more. The more you know, the more you want to know. It's a never-ending growth process.

Act--Do something, take action. For some reason I envision this category as a movie-making experience: lights, camera, action. Unfortunately, there are no retakes in the game of real life. Take action, get results. The results may be good, bad, or neutral, but at least there are results if you take action. I define action as something we choose to do to further our mission. Prayer and learning come first, since they give us direction and knowledge that will help guide our actions. They give us the courage and wisdom to understand what we should continue, start, or stop doing. Action items are anything you do that is in line with your mission, outside of the other PLAY categories.

Write down anything that you labeled as a valuable activity in your baseline that is not more appropriately classified as pray, learn, or youthify. You may want to read about youthify below first, and then come back. Also list actions you would like to start or stop. For those of you going to school or working, many of your actions might be set by others. Go with those unless they significantly interfere with your God-given mission. You really don't have to get too carried away with these classifications. I realize there are overlaps in the categories. For instance, if you are in school, your actions are mainly about learning. I'd classify class time and homework time as action. Then I'd count anything else that I was studying outside of school as learning. Make sense? Remember our basic principle: Keep it simple.

Youthify--Keep yourself energized. Maintain your youthful attitude forever. A younger friend of mine calls me "the youngest old guy he's ever met." I like that and he swears it's a compliment. Do activities that people associate with younger people. Try new things. Move more and eat less. Drink water. Floss. Smile. Laugh. Find a hobby. Play games with human interaction. Get a pet. Spend time with supportive family and friends. In other words, take care of your physical and emotional health. Spiritual and mental health are taken care of by praying and learning. Financial health will be taken care of by your actions. So you now have the complete health package.

Quick point of emphasis: Our number-one priority is to take care of ourselves. Without our health, everything becomes much more difficult. Please put some form of daily exercise at the top of your youthify list--just 30 minutes of something, anything that gets you moving around. And eat to live, don't live to eat.

Make a list of all the activities you would like to pursue to keep yourself young and energized. Again, list them all without judgment or without focusing on constraints. You will have your chance to get real later.

Everything else--Finally let's talk about the catch-all, everything-else category. Any activity that is not valuable to advancing our mission belongs in the everything-else category. You may try to justify many things under the Youthify category to avoid calling them wasteful, especially entertainment-type activities such as TV, video games, sporting events, parties, and the list goes on. I ask myself, What is the primary reason I am doing this, and how much is enough for each of those activities? TV is my problem. I'm counting it all as waste right now. Maybe watching an hour a day with my spouse is valuable? These decisions are up to you. My advice is to keep pure entertainment to a minimum. Let your conscience be your guide.

Rest--If you are investing your time wisely in the PLAY categories, you will no doubt sleep well. Get what you need. Eight hours is recommended by most experts. You may need less, but you probably don't need more.

That's it, six categories to track. Really just four, since tracking sleep and putting the remainder in everything else isn't that difficult. They represent all the important right things you can do in life to make a positive difference in the world. Use the Playtime Tracker, which can be found in the Sandbox to record your time. And yes, now you can go out and play.

Summary –

- The major categories of right things form the acronym PLAYER:
  - Pray
  - Learn
  - Act
  - Youthify
  - Everything else
  - Rest
- The first four are the valuable activities that will enable us to achieve our mission. They will be referred to as PLAY from here on.

Actions Items –

- Use the Potential PLAY Activities worksheet in the Sandbox to make a starter list of things you would like to do in each category.
- Choose one new item from your list and start it in the upcoming week.
- Use the individual letters in PLAY to categorize your calendar activities in the upcoming week.
- Any activity that doesn't fit in the PLAY categories gets an "E" for everything else, except for rest which gets an "R."
- Record your time at the end of each day in the upcoming week on the Playtime Tracker form.
- Total your hours and compute the averages on the Playtime Tracker at the end of the week.

15

PLAYTIME GOALS

D ID YOU TRACK your time last week into the PLAY categories using the Playtime Tracker (PTT) to establish a new baseline? No doubt you noticed that the form has a column labeled "goal" that we haven't used yet. Now that we have tracked our daily activity for a couple weeks and have a good feel for how you have been investing your time, let's set some time-allocation goals. The goals we establish will assist us to create the habit of investing most of our time in activities that are valuable in carrying out our mission.

This simple step may be your key to attaining eternal life. Sound dramatic? It really can be a life-changing and -gaining experience. And you will be done with this in less than a half hour. Ready, set, go.

Do you really need the data you have collected about how you currently spend your time in order to set future goals? No, but it does help in understanding the degree of change you will be committing to. Let's start by setting a rest goal. Most experts agree that the ideal amount of sleep needed is eight hours. Choose a number that gives you the rest you need to be at your peak performance.

Next, decide the percentage of your waking hours that you want to spend on PLAY activities. I chose 80 percent. Not easy, given that I started at way under 50 percent. Eighty percent of 16 hours rounds up to 13 hours a day. This is a big stretch, yet certainly achievable. It's going to take some time to break old habits, so I'm setting weekly improvement goals to get there over time. You may want to do this as well: Set a big-stretch goal that you can work up to. I find this a better motivational strategy than setting something that is too easily achieved.

Look at your daily average column in the total PLAY row of last week's PTT. Divide that number by your total awake average number. The result is your current percentage of time spent on PLAY activities. Or as I think of it, your valuable investment of time. My pre-goal-setting result was 7/16, about 44 percent. This is better than the initial 38 percent, but still sad. Calculate yours, then set your overall PLAY percentage goal.

Almost there. Aren't numbers fun? Multiply your PLAY goal percentage by your total daily awake hours. If you are using eight hours for sleep, your awake hours are 16: 24 hours in a day minus 8 for sleep. My calculation is 80 percent x 16 hours = about 13 hours per day. Calculate yours.

Last step. Allocate your overall PLAY hours goal to the PLAY categories. For me, that means spreading the 13 daily hours out to prayer, learning, taking action, and youthifing. My thinking went like this:

- I should spend at least as much time on action as I do sleeping. Act - 8 hours
- Surely I can give God at least one hour a day in prayer. Pray – 1 hour
- I have a lot to learn in order to achieve my new mission. Learn - 2 hours
- I need to keep myself healthy and energized. Youthify - 2 hours
- Total = 13 hours per day

To make this happen, I will need to cut my everything-else hours in half. That is going to be really difficult, requiring a tremendous exercise of self-discipline. But I also know it will be rewarding and that I will regret it forever if I don't take this seriously. I'm in, let's go!

Your turn. Allocate your overall daily PLAY hours' goal. You may want to establish two sets of goals: one to use immediately and one you really want to achieve over a set period of time. I gave myself three months to get to the 80-percent goal mentioned above. I started at 50 percent and increased it weekly. I don't always get to 13 hours, but after three months, I'm averaging over 10, which is a huge improvement from my starting point of 6. Progress feels so good!

Simply taking the time to establish goals and measure progress drives rapid improvement. I'm in a constant battle between the Act and Everything-else categories. Of course, I realize that my time is not directed by others at this point, except of course by my precious spouse and energetic puppies. You might not be so lucky yet. If you are working and raising a family, I'm sure your playtime total is fairly high already. I recall our everything-else time being virtually nonexistent during those years. But the valuable hours from a mission perspective were quite low, unless the mission was make a living. Let's just say it was.

A last quick word about school and work hours. Count them all as Act for now, but also take some time to consider how many of them are valuable from a God-given mission perspective. For me, it was probably something like 20 percent. Then again, without all that experience, I might not be doing this today. Only He knows for sure. I really hope that as part of the decision-making process at the pearly gates, we all get the opportunity for a true life review. I would love to know what my mission truly was, what key decisions I should have made along the way, and what the results of those choices would have been. It would be interesting to know what could have been. Might be depressing, but I'd like to know.

Wouldn't you? Hopefully it will be close enough to what I actually did to be looked upon favorably (close like horseshoes, not hand grenades).

Enough talk, set your time-allocation goals so we can move on to determining what specifically we should do with that time. In the meantime, your assignment for the upcoming week is to strive to adhere to your new time-allocation goals. You can do it!

SUMMARY –

- Motivating goals help to focus your time and energy.
- Allocate your time wisely into mission-relevant activities.
- Setting goals and measuring results drives rapid improvement.

ACTION ITEMS –

- Use your PTT from last week to help you establish your new play-time-allocation goals.
- Print a new PTT for the upcoming week, and write in your new goals.
- Review your upcoming schedule in light of these new goals, and adjust it as needed.
- Complete the PTT daily, and review it against your time-allocation goals.
- Total your hours at the end of the week, and compare the averages to your goals.
- Identify what you did well and what you could improve upon.

16

PLAYGROUND PLAN

THE PLAYGROUND WAS my favorite spot on the planet as a kid. Sandbox, swings, slides, kickball, scatterball, wiffleball, tetherball, sand--what's not to like? I think I first learned about planning in anticipation of recess. I spent every free minute of class time plotting our fun-time activities. Teams were set before the much awaited bell even rang. Ring, run, go. There will be no wasted time on the playground! Same concept here. We need a solid plan for how we are going to spend the time we allocated to each PLAY category, so we won't waste any valuable playtime.

Squirrel! I noticed in my later years of work that the new crop of college grads weren't very good at planning. I assumed that was because at some point, adults began planning their whole lives for them. We put them in organized activities very early in life. They have a coach, set times to practice and play, nice facilities, and officials to enforce the rules. And trophies, don't forget the participation prizes for all. Back in the day, we did all that by ourselves. Except the trophies; the prize was participation. We planned our own fun; we had to after our parents insisted that the weather was too nice to be indoors. Even then, we usually had to walk uphill, into the wind, through snow, sleet, and ice to get to our rendezvous point. And we liked it! Oh, and we had no parent fights in the stands, since they weren't invited. (Have I mentioned that I coached travel ice hockey teams for several years? Stories for another time.)

There is no time to waste on the playground. Let's make a plan now. There are two tools in the Sandbox for your use. The first, PLAY Plan Options (PPO), is a starter list of potential activities to consider within each PLAY category. It lists what you could do, as well as when, where, and how you could do them. You should also refer to the lists you made earlier for each category on the Potential PLAY Activities form.

Use the PLAYground Activity Tracker (PAT), the second tool, to capture what you decide and commit to doing in the upcoming week. For each category, start with the things you already do and want to continue. Determine how much time those activities will take. Then add new items to fill in the time you have allocated to each category.

I could spend a lot of time describing this process in detail, and I probably would if I were still working, in order to meet the weight test. You know, to make sure a work product looks substantial enough that people will assume you worked hard and have obviously thought everything through. Of course no one would read it all. That's why God invented the executive summary. At least a few will read that, but most will wait for the presentation. I have a friend who would insert the line, "tell me you read this and I'll buy you a coke" in his reports. Last I heard he has never had to pay up. That tells you something.

You are all obviously smart people. You will figure it out and adapt it to your liking. I'll spare you the detail and merely provide a quick example. Take a look at the PPO. Your task is to pick the what, when, where, and how in each category that will achieve your time-allocation goals. The items listed in the various columns are independent of each other. Simply choose one item from each column within a category to develop one planned activity. For instance, one of my Pray plan activities is to say the rosary, over lunch, in my office using an app I have on my phone. (Maybe we should develop a card game where you pick one card from each column and do that for a day? Or not.) I have an hour allocated to prayer. The rosary takes about 20 minutes. I added 20-minute morning and evening prayers to round out the full hour. Make sense?

Two more things: When you have completed your PAT, make sure that your plan is on your schedule. Not that you have to write all the PAT items on your calendar, but you need to make sure they fit within the schedule. Get creative. For example, if you have at least a 20-minute commute to work, you have time to say the rosary. My wife's car is like a shrine to prayer. Initially I claimed this likely led to distracted driving. She asserts it enhances her driving as she is more calm resulting in compassionate driving and no urge toward road rage. Upon experimentation I found this to be true and her to be right once again. And interesting to note, she's never caused an accident or been given a ticket. Pulled over yes, ticket no. I think the authorities are afraid of the possible consequences.

Go ahead and complete your PAT for the upcoming week and get the activities on your schedule.

Important note. Planning is important; doing is essential. Plans mean nothing unless you actually carry them out. Now that your plan is built and on your schedule, it's time to track what you actually do. Continue to mark your calendar activities, using the appropriate play category letter. At the end of each day, record your hours on the PLAYtime Tracker (PTT). Also, complete the PAT by checking off the various activities completed that day. Briefly review both reports. Take a minute to feel good about your successes and note any improvement opportunities. Look at your schedule for the next day, and make any needed changes. I just timed myself doing this. Slightly under 3 minutes. No excuses, make it happen!

CONGRATULATIONS! you have completed your personal "Right Things" plan to support your mission. Very impressive! You are now consciously investing your time wisely in pursuit of your mission. You know what you want to do, and you are actually doing it. Way to go!

We are now in control of the RT component of our saint-building formula (RT x RW x G = S). Time to move on to learning about the "Right Way" and developing our complementary plan in that regard.

SUMMARY –

- We need a plan in order to invest our time wisely.
- The activities in our plan must be on our schedule.
- Track your actual activities and time daily.
- Review results and make necessary adjustments to continuously improve.

ACTION ITEMS –

- Review the PLAYground Plan Options document.
- Add your own ideas to the lists.
- Choose what you would like to do in each section.
- Complete the PLAYground Activity Tracker.
- Ensure that your planned activities are on your schedule for the upcoming week.
- Indicate on your calendar which P-L-A-Y category each activity falls into.
- Summarize your time on the PTT and check off your activities on the PAT at the end of each day.
- Review your results and plan for the next day.
- Update your PAT and your schedule at the beginning of each week as you deem necessary.

PART 5

THE RIGHT WAY

17

CHOICES

B EFORE DELVING INTO the Right Way topic, let's talk choices. We discussed habits prior to talking about the Right Things. Hopefully, we have begun the habit of investing our time wisely: doing small things daily that will grow exponentially over time into significant results. Habits will keep us on the path to success; wise choices will ensure that we are actually on the right path. Every choice or decision we make has three possible outcomes: It keeps us on the right path, puts us on the wrong path, or causes us to veer off course temporarily. As you know, the right path is the one that moves us closer to accomplishing our mission.

Up to this point, we have mainly been discussing things we will be doing, and we have made some choices that have placed us on the right path. Our next topic focuses on the behaviors we should exhibit while doing these things. We will face numerous daily choices about how we go about conducting our business in the world. This is when things get really difficult--not because they should be difficult, but because our current culture has made them so. Specifically, the culture of relativity successfully blurs the line between right and wrong. Fighting this will be our most significant daily struggle in carrying out our mission, but we can succeed by supporting each other.

I believe we all know right from wrong instinctively. It was easier when we are kids, but we still know as adults. We usually choose right, but there are times when we don't. Sometimes we don't think through the consequences of our actions completely, or we may want something so badly that we find reasons to justify our bad behavior. Often, these poor choices happen unconsciously and unintentionally, but unfortunately, we still have to live with the consequences. We may not even realize that other people may be affected by our choices too. The point is, the sum total of our choices becomes the sum total of our life. They make or break us.

Thinking back to the happiness index exercise, I realize that both the ups and downs were the result of my choices. All the difficult times were self-inflicted. Of course at the time, I was wondering why this was happening to me. We are all a product of our choices. If our choices are in line with our God-given mission and with doing what's right, we become happier and more holy. If not, things go in the opposite direction, and we harm ourselves, and probably others too.

The trouble is that frequently it's hard to understand at decision time which direction a particular choice will take us. And often we don't let the simple principles of right and wrong guide our decision making. If only we could plug each choice option into a computer that could give us the answer. But there is something we can do. Two simple questions might be all we need to ask each time we have a choice to make: (a) Is what I am about to do moving me closer to accomplishing my mission, and (b) can I do it in a moral way? I'll state what I believe again: Discovering and acting upon our mission in a moral way is the key to pursuing sainthood. *Disclaimer: I could be wrong, but what does it hurt to try to maximize our potential for the benefit of others in a holy way? Oh, and praying to God to grant us His Grace!*

So how can we make sure we more consistently make the right choices? Doing right simply because we know it's the right way to live doesn't seem to work. We need a bigger reason, a daily motivation to always do

right. How about this choice, heaven or hell? Most studies of human behavior conclude that we are more highly motivated by fear than by desire,
so let's talk a little fear.

What is the worst possible thing you can imagine happening to you?
Think things like death, illness, incarceration, torture, etc. Or imagine
yourself in an unbelievably cruel living situation. All anyone really needs
to do is get on the internet or listen to the news to learn about horrible
things happening to others across the world. Place yourself in their situation. Or read a book about the Holocaust or some political revolution
where hundreds of thousands, even millions of people were murdered
and worse. Now, know that hell is worse than anything we can experience here on earth, worse than anything our minds can imagine. And
know that you will experience it FOREVER! If we truly believed this, we
would all be highly motivated to live saintly lives. But apparently we
don't, because we aren't.

Is this enough fear to guide your decisions along the right path?
Or will you just avoid thinking about it? Avoidance of anything always
catches up to you. The desire to go to heaven and live there for an eternity should be enough motivation for us all. It's way more enjoyable to
think about the best things that you can imagine happening to yourself.
Heaven will be infinitely better than that! Enough said.

Take some time to think about both possible outcomes. Make them
real for yourself. They are in fact reality for us all. Actually, some people think neither is real. I suppose they could be right, but why take a
chance? Anyway, there is enough motivation for nearly all of us to choose
good over evil, right over wrong, and to know that both those extremes
do exist. Of course, just because we know we should do right doesn't
mean we will. For that we need inspiration and grace.

Inspiration is what makes us actually want to do something versus just
knowing we should. It helps us go beyond thoughts to take action in a

positive direction. For me, it is usually driven by seeing what someone else has done or is doing. Then I know it's possible for me too. For you, it may be something else: reading inspirational quotes, books, or articles; going to mass every day; going to reconciliation frequently to be inspired by the grace of forgiveness and the desire to do better; being around other people with a similar desire to become saints. It may be all of the above. Personally, I need constant reminding, as the world has made it so much easier to be a sinner than a winner.

Have you ever been looked at strangely for being kind? It's always amazing to me that I'm sometimes viewed suspiciously for being nice to people--just common courtesy-type actions. Smile, say hello, hold a door open, give a compliment, and ask if assistance is needed. Try it and see what kind of looks and comments you get. I've actually had people get angry at my attempts to be kind.

Recently, I've been trying to talk with people in the gym. Nearly everyone has headphones on, and few speak to each other. Eye contact is minimal. It's like watching some zombie movie. They all just mill around, moving from one machine to the next. A few will engage in minimal conversation. Overall I think I'm viewed as an annoyance by men and a creep by women. I'd love to do a study on that someday. I've decided I don't care, and I'm going to continue to be friendly. Eventually maybe they will know I'm sincere. Or maybe I should wear a priest's collar so they assume that in the first place. Is there some sort of spiritual penalty for impersonating a priest? Never mind, it just can't be a good idea.

Enough about choices; you get the picture. Just know you will need to find what motivates and inspires you as we move on. Help is on the way later. Just wanted to get you thinking about it now.

18

RULES, RULES AND MORE RULES

H OW MANY RULES do you have to follow every day? Do you think it is even possible to count them any more? Let's see, we have federal, state, and local laws. Each of them have rules and regulations. Then we have household, workplace, school, and even neighborhood rules.

I worked in a heavily regulated industry for most of my career. In the beginning most of the rules made logical sense. Now many are only logical if you trace them back to their origin. It has become nearly impossible to comply with them all. For example, the U.S. federal tax code began as 400 pages in 1913. By 1981, when I started my CPA career, it was about 25,000 pages, and it tripled in size during my working years to over 75,000 pages. Wow!

What's this got to do with anything? I used to like rules. They bring structure and order to our lives and are necessary to avoid chaos. But it has gotten a little out of control. How about we get back to the basics? The natural laws of right and wrong that are so basic that we all know them instinctively from birth. Then we unlearn them as we age in order to get what we want and justify our behaviors. These laws are all logical and based on common sense. To me, following them constitutes the "Right Way."

Over time, I had become confused about what the right way was. It seemed easy when I was a kid but became increasingly abstract as life went on. I want it to be simple again, as I think it was meant to be. After much research, I have come to my personal conclusion on the rules of the right way. I offer it to you for consideration.

I actually thought this would be an easy research task, since our shared purpose is to strive to become saints. Just go to the source: God. What is the first thing you think of? The Ten Commandments, right? They were God's way of making His expectations explicit, since the people at the time of Moses were driving Him crazy. He had to be thinking, "I keep saving you people, and all you do is complain and do stupid stuff--come on!" Not much has changed for Him, I'm guessing. We are very sorry! If He weren't God, He'd be really frustrated. Since He is, I bet He laughs a lot. Anyway, here are the Ten Commandments:

1. I am the Lord your God; you shall not have strange gods before me.
2. You shall not take the name of the Lord your God in vain.
3. Remember to keep holy the Lord's day.
4. Honor your father and your mother.
5. You shall not kill.
6. You shall not commit adultery.
7. You shall not steal.
8. You shall not bear false witness against your neighbor.
9. You shall not covet your neighbor's wife.
10. You shall not covet your neighbor's goods.

This is obviously a great list: two things to do and eight things not to do. Seems simple enough. But there's more. In the Sermon on the Mount, Jesus gave us a list of how we can be blessed:

THE BEATITUDES

1. Blessed are the poor in spirit, for theirs is the kingdom of heaven.
2. Blessed are those who mourn, for they will be comforted.
3. Blessed are the meek, for they will inherit the earth.
4. Blessed are those who hunger and thirst for righteousness, for they will be filled.
5. Blessed are the merciful, for they will receive mercy.
6. Blessed are the pure in heart, for they will see God.
7. Blessed are the peacemakers, for they will be called children of God.
8. Blessed are those who are persecuted for righteousness' sake, for theirs is the kingdom of heaven.

Then there are the works of mercy, which I recall learning long ago. I looked them up and found many consistent versions but had trouble finding an exact origin. I gave up trying, since it really doesn't matter. Let's just say they are all in the Bible in various locations and call it good.

THE CORPORAL WORKS OF MERCY

1. Harbor the homeless.
2. Feed the hungry.
3. Give drink to the thirsty.
4. Clothe the naked.
5. Visit the sick.
6. Ransom the captive.
7. Bury the dead.

THE SPIRITUAL WORKS OF MERCY

1. Comfort the afflicted.
2. Instruct the ignorant.

3. Counsel the doubtful.
4. Admonish the sinner.
5. Bear wrongs patiently.
6. Forgive offenses willingly.
7. Pray for the living and the dead.

Adding them all together, we now have 32 rules. It's getting more confusing, especially since some are rules to be obeyed and some are more like suggestions. Just for fun, I googled "New Testament rules." The first item in the search results was titled, "1,050 New Testament Commands." I took a quick look to find out that some organization had identified that many Bible verses and even broken them down into 69 major headings. Wow! It looked really interesting. I'll get back to it someday. Personally I think even 32 rules is too many. I learned long ago that most of us can only retain things in small lists: 3, 5, or 7 at the most. Let's keep searching.

How about the Old Testament? Wikipedia says it contains 613 laws. Quick squirrel: My favorite quote about this source came from the character Michael Scott on the hit show *The Office*. He said, ""Wikipedia is the best thing ever. Anyone in the world can write anything they want, so you know you are getting the best possible information." Priceless. I seem to recall that many of the 613 laws required sacrificing things; count me out! Have you ever read those detailed rules? Who says God doesn't have a sense of humor? He must have been thinking, "Wow, they couldn't stop themselves from eating the forbidden apple, but they are actually attempting to follow these ridiculous rules I created just to amuse myself. These people are so gullible! Wait, I created them in my own image. Ah whatever, you gotta be able to laugh at yourself."

Can we please get down to just a few? Yes, we can! The greatest commandments. There are only two, as spoken by Jesus and recorded in Matthew 22:35. Let's repeat it one more time.

You shall love the Lord, your God, with all your heart, with all your soul, with all your mind. This is the greatest and the first commandment. And the second is like it: You shall love your neighbor as yourself.

By living these two commandments, we would likely be living the other 32 or 1,050 as well. Love God and love your neighbors. By the way, "neighbors" are defined as everyone else on the planet. This is certainly easy to remember. You learned it in the Quick Start. How have you been doing? Yeah, it's tough.

I've always found the last two words of the commandment interesting, "as yourself." I know many people who don't necessarily love themselves. Do they only have to love others to that extent? What if they actually hate themselves? Is it then okay to hate others? Isn't that kind of what actually happens naturally? Our treatment of others is typically a reflection of our feelings about ourselves? (Wow, that's deep, Scott. Someone else must be typing this.) What about the often quoted Golden Rule? Let's look that up. Well, isn't that convenient. It's also found in Matthew, 7:12 to be exact: **"Do to others whatever you would have them do to you."** Again, I have similar questions. I'm going to attempt to treat others better than I treat myself, just to be on the safe side.

Maybe these two commandments are a little too broad--or just too hard. I always thought my business claim to fame was the ability to find and fix the root cause of problems. This is the only way to ensure the problem is solved for good. If you only treat the symptoms, not the cause, the problem will come back to haunt you.

So let's remind ourselves, What is the problem that we are trying to solve? Sin. What is sin? The Ten Commandments were given to us as a guideline to avoid sin. Not following them is therefore sin, right? But what are the underlying reasons we commit those sins, the root causes? Good question! Ever hear of the Seven Deadly Sins? I think even nonreligious types could name a couple of them. After another round of research, I am convinced that they are the root cause of sin. Take my word for it, or read this book, *Seven Deadly Sins*, by Kevin Vost. It is a fascinating history lesson on how the sins were identified and eventually came to number seven. You won't find them in the Bible. The seven sins can be broadly classified as vices. Thankfully, there are also seven virtues that serve to combat those vices. Vost's book also contains battle plans to defeat each vice. Check it out once you get further into fighting the good fight.

The many versions of the seven sins vary in wording and order. I've settled on the following, since the terms seemed like they would be easily recognizable and understood with little explanation.

Seven Deadly Sins (Vices)	Seven Contrary Virtues
1. Pride	1. Humility
2. Greed	2. Charity
3. Envy	3. Kindness
4. Anger	4. Patience
5. Lust	5. Chastity
6. Gluttony	6. Temperance
7. Sloth	7. Diligence

The next chapter includes definitions. For now, just think about ways in which you currently exhibit each of them, assuming you do, of course.

Do you still need convincing that the vices are in fact the root cause of sin? Here is one of the exercises I did to convince myself. I matched the vices as reasons for breaking The Ten Commandments. My question for each was, What vice could cause me to break this commandment? Here is the result. I did this quickly as a test; please don't judge my answers too harshly. Try it for yourself.

Commandment	Commandment-Breaking Vices
1. I am the Lord your God; you shall not have strange gods before me.	Pride, Envy, Anger
2. You shall not take the name of the Lord your God in vain.	Pride, Envy, Anger
3. Remember to keep holy the Lord's day.	Pride, Greed
4. Honor your father and your mother.	Pride, Anger, Sloth
5. You shall not kill.	Pride, Greed, Envy, Anger
6. You shall not commit adultery.	Pride, Envy, Anger, Lust
7. You shall not steal.	Pride, Greed, Envy, Anger
8. You shall not bear false witness against your neighbor.	Pride, Greed, Envy, Anger, Sloth
9. You shall not covet your neighbor's wife.	Pride, Envy, Anger, Lust
10. You shall not covet your neighbor's goods.	Pride, Envy, Anger, Gluttony, Sloth

My conclusions were that (a) the vices are in fact the root causes of sin, and (b) pride is the worst, appearing as the vice causing every commandment to be broken.

The "Right Way" is therefore to conduct our daily business by exhibiting the virtues and avoiding the vices. Are you with me? Need further definitions? Moving on.

19

VICE/VIRTUE

L ET'S EXPLORE EACH vice and contrary virtue in a little more depth. Putting these two "V" terms next to each other made me think of the term, vice versa. Its definition is "with the reverse order, the other way around." That's interesting; I have a natural tendency to think about avoiding the negative rather than focusing on the positive. Maybe we should do the opposite. Rather than placing our energy on avoiding the vices, how about we focus on living the virtues? Over time, the vices should just fade away from our lives due to the lack of attention--the old "out of sight, out of mind" strategy.

Now, I'm thinking about the age-old sports debate of what makes for the best team, a great offense or a great defense. All arguments have their merits, and in the end, I think the real answer is that it depends. I could go on for a long time on this topic, but I'll spare you. Instead I'll simply give you my personal conclusion as it relates to the topic at hand.

It seems to me that the devil is focusing on offense, based on the cultural slide away from virtuous behaviors. Personally, it sure feels like those of us trying to live the moral high ground are constantly on defense. Having your defense on the field most of the time is exhausting;

you are always reacting. The offense knows exactly what they are going to do. The defense has to recognize what is happening and figure out how best to defend against it. This is both mentally and physically taxing.

Since we seem to be losing the defensive battle, it's time for a change in strategy. I've come to the conclusion that we must concentrate on playing offense. Let's focus on the positives, the virtues. Who's with me? It's time to focus our energy on proactively and persistently living the virtues. The enemy will continue to tempt us with the vices, but we can overcome with a little self-discipline. More on that later. First, let's be clear on what we are fighting for and against.

I make no claim of expertise on the virtues and vices, other than having read about them extensively and having experienced them firsthand in real life. The brief descriptions below, which pair virtues with their contrary vices, are simple dictionary definitions, helpful synonyms, and some commentary that helped in my own understanding.

Virtue--Moral excellence and righteousness; goodness. Integrity, honesty, uprightness.

Vice--A practice or habit considered to be evil, degrading, or immoral. Depravity, iniquity, corruption, badness, wickedness, sin, weakness.

Diligence--Careful and persistent work or effort. Conscientiousness, dedication, commitment, tenacity. Doing what you were meant to do with passion. Making a positive difference for the benefit of others. Taking action. Being proactive. Focusing your efforts on important work. Avoiding distractions. Determination and persistence in pursuit of worthwhile goals. Living your mission.

Sloth--Reluctance to work or make an effort. Laziness, idleness, inactivity, inertia, sluggishness, shiftlessness, apathy, listlessness, lethargy. Not doing what you are supposed to be doing. Alternatively, doing what you are not supposed to do. Not doing the good you know you should do, or doing nothing worthwhile at all, that is, nothing meaningful or useful to achieving your mission. I guess technically we are always doing something. Unless it involves committing some sin, I'm pretty sure that doing something is always better than doing nothing. At least you are living. (Oh, one more thing, another definition of sloth for trivia purposes is a group of bears.)

Temperance--Self-restraint in action. Self-control, self-discipline, self-denial, abstinence, moderation. Abstinence from certain food and drink, based on self-control. Moderation in all things.
Gluttony--An inordinate desire to consume more than what one requires. Overeating, insatiability, piggishness, voraciousness. Living to eat versus eating to live. Drinking and maybe drugging your worries away. According to a 2013 study by Mayo Clinic and Olmsted Medical Center researchers, nearly 70 percent of Americans are on at least one prescription drug, and more than half take two. Antibiotics, antidepressants, and painkilling opioids are most commonly prescribed. How about this? More than two thirds of adults are considered to be overweight or obese. The estimated annual health-care costs of obesity-related illness are nearly 21% of annual medical spending in the United States. Sad!

Chastity--The state or quality of being chaste; moral purity. Celibacy, purity, innocence, abstinence, virtue in both thoughts and actions.
Lust--An inordinate craving for the pleasures of the body. Intense desire, passion, yearning, longing, lasciviousness. I thought about looking up statistics about sexually transmitted diseases, abortions, pornography, and divorce, but I really don't want to know. We all know these are big problems. Enough said.

Patience--The capacity to endure pain, difficulty, provocation, or annoyance with calm. Tolerance, restraint, composure, indulgence, resoluteness, fortitude, serenity, stamina. Think before you react. Serenity now.

Wrath--Angry, violent, or stern indignation. Anger is manifested in the individual who spurns love and opts instead for fury. Anger, rage, fury, outrage, displeasure, annoyance, irritation, ire, madness.

Kindness--The quality of being friendly, generous, and considerate. Caring, helpful, thoughtful, unselfish, selfless, altruistic, compassionate, sympathetic, understanding, big-hearted, benevolent, friendly, hospitable, neighborly.

Envy--A feeling of discontent or resentment aroused by a desire for someone else's possessions, abilities, status, or situation. Jealousy, covetousness, resentment, bitterness, discontent, the green-eyed monster. Comparing yourself to others.

Charity--The voluntary giving of help to those in need. Kindness and tolerance in judging others. Aid, relief, alms, philanthropy, benevolence, goodwill, compassion, consideration, concern, kindness, sympathy, indulgence, tolerance, leniency.

Greed--Extreme desire for wealth or material gain. Covetousness, materialism. Also known as avarice; insatiable desire for riches; inordinate miserly desire to gain and hoard wealth. Acquisitiveness, cupidity, selfishness, miserliness, stinginess. Often driven by a desire to show superiority over others.

Humility--A modest opinion of one's own importance. Modest, humble, servile, respectful, deferential. Thinking of others first. Often viewed as a weakness in today's culture.

Pride--An excessively high opinion of oneself. Narcissism, vanity, vainglory, arrogance, conceit, bigheadedness, smugness, self-importance, egotism, superiority, immodesty. An excessive belief in one's own abilities that interferes with one's recognition of the grace of God. It has been called the sin from which all others arise. Elevating self, judging and criticizing others, bragging, degrading, insisting on doing it my way. (Trivia version: a group of lions forming a social unit.)

One other interesting note on pride and its place in our culture. The first two dictionary definitions I found were positive: (a) a sense of one's own proper dignity or value; self-respect, and (b) pleasure or satisfaction taken in an achievement, possession, or association. Tells you something. It was the only vice that had an alternate positive meaning. Do you think that's a coincidence? The worst is also the best?

Going forward, I'm just going to refer to virtues and vices collectively as V's to make it simple. As I progressed down the list, it seemed to me that further explanations are really not necessary. I was going to point out the problems in our society that are evidence of each vice, but it was getting really depressing so I stopped. If you want more, let me know. I also looked for a few statistics to support the virtues, and they were harder to locate. Here's one: The average charitable contribution per U.S. household per year is almost $3,000. Let's leave on this high note.

20

THE DEEPEST ROOT

B EFORE WE MOVE on, let me offer one more thought on the root cause of sin. As discussed in the last chapter, the vices are the root cause of sin, and the virtues are our way to combat those vices. It is completely up to us which path we choose in every situation we encounter. We are free to choose our own thoughts, words, and actions. It follows, therefore, that we are actually the deepest root cause of sin. Each and every one of us is a problem unto ourselves. We live in a selfish society that promotes the vices; they sprout from the root of "me first." The virtues are all "others first" focused. Remember the greatest commandments? If we truly want to experience joy in our lives, we need to think, speak, and act "JOY": Jesus, Others, and You, in that order. Only by adopting a Jesus-and-Others-first mentality can we consistently live the virtues. In fact, it is the only way we will succeed in our pursuit of sainthood.

Have you learned how to juggle yet? Come on! Find three balls. Label them "J," "O," and "Y." Check out the instructional video I made for you at saintbuilder.com. You will learn how to juggle in just over two minutes. Start with one ball, add the second, and finally add the third. Of course you will start with the J ball, add the O, and then the Y. Say the words out loud when you toss each ball. By the time you succeed, you will never forget the meaning and order of JOY. Plus, you will impress your friends with your new-found talent. You can do it! I won't be asking again. You're welcome.

Having a joyful life should be so easy. Living virtues over vices will always produce more joy. The problem is that vices have a greater ability to produce near-term pleasure. In an "I-want-it-now" society, that is trouble and likely to result in immediate joy and eventual sadness. Vices are constantly promoted in our culture, and they seem to be the much easier choice. Don't you find it strange that you often have to explain why you are doing something that is virtuous? Choosing vice rarely seems to need defending.

Here's a ridiculous example: I don't use dressing on salads because I don't like the taste and there is really no nutritional value in it. Every time I order a plain salad, I get a disapproving question and "the look" from the wait staff and sometimes dinner companions. You know the look, the one you fear from your Mom or spouse. Choosing temperance in ordering a salad is obviously not a big virtue, especially since I'd let them put sugar on it if that were an option. It's just that the norm in dining out is gluttony. You get the same look for not ordering drinks and a dessert. Now apply that dumb example to important things like premarital sex, drinking, drugs, etc. Aren't you more likely to get questions and the look for not doing those things? Just go along to get along. Or not!

Want more proof that vices are winning? More than 640,000 self-help books exist. My bet is that most of them promote choosing virtue over vice in some way or another. They don't use those terms, but that is in essence what they are recommending. One of my favorites was the very popular The 7 Habits of Highly Effective People, by Stephen Covey. Those seven habits are not the seven virtues, but they each contain elements of them. Check it out sometime. Our habits make or break us.

My next point was going to be that there are no self-help books on vices. Wrong! All sorts of books teach us how to master vices, with more than 18,000 focusing on gambling alone. My belief is that virtues come to us naturally as children; they are ingrained in us from birth. Then, for some reason, they become increasingly hard to practice consistently. Yet a magnetic force always seems to be trying to pull us back to them. And we are naturally happier when we are virtuous.

Vices are learned over time. Encouraged by our culture, they creep into our behavior as we age. They give us moments of pleasure but ultimately lead to pain. Vices are one bad decision away and may take twelve steps to eventually overcome. Isn't the first step admitting we have a problem? We do all have a problem; we sin. It's time to work on our sin-reduction strategy.

The strategy starts and ends with me, with my choices and behavior. I need to get control of myself. Don't we all? How do we do that? Through self-discipline and self-denial. Start with small decisions. Basically we make choices to do or not to do something. I decided to start denying myself one small thing daily. My hope was that success in denial of little things would result in an ability to do the same with big things over time. Actually I chose denial of one thing I wanted to do and one I didn't. For instance, I want a candy bar as a reward for all this writing. I have one nearby, but I'm going to resist. I also don't want to walk the dogs right now, but they are staring at me. Fine, let's go.

21

EXAMINATION OF
CONSCIENCE

I T'S TIME TO establish a baseline on how we are doing in using the virtues to battle the vices. Let's use a scoring system to make it interesting. I introduce you to the Flying V Tracker (FVT), which you can find in the Sandbox. We will use it to score our daily performance. Why the weird name? Remember how I overcame my desire to not walk the dogs? Well, as we were strolling along, I pondered what to call this score sheet. I knew it should have a V in it, but nothing interesting was coming to mind. Suddenly, a gaggle of geese flying in a V formation was overhead. I had two thoughts: (a) don't look up! and (b) thanks for the sign, God. Those geese were working together to soar on their journey, and so will we. Good walk timing, puppies.

The tracker has a row for each virtue and each vice, as well as columns for each day of the week. There are also rows and columns for totals and for a net daily and weekly score. Wouldn't it be cool if there was a wearable spiritual device? Rather than tracking your steps, it would track each time you demonstrated one of the V's. The main purpose of those devices is to create awareness of our activities, and that's what we want too. I have an app design in mind to help us. For now, just carry the paper FVT and a pen.

I think of tracking the V's as a game. When we play the game, our virtuous self battles against our sinful self. You could also think of it as you versus the devil. But saying "the devil made me do it" is not a valid excuse. You made you do it. Think of your opponent however you want. Personally, I like thinking of my enemy as someone other than myself, even though I know the truth. Let's dance, satan! (Spell check tells me that name is supposed to be capitalized, but I refuse to do that!)

You score points by exhibiting one of the virtues or vices in your daily moments of truth, those decision points where you could choose one or the other. These moments happen all day long, starting with the wake-up alarm. Are you going to get up and get moving (diligence), or are you going to hit the snooze (sloth)? It's up to you how detailed you want to get with this. At first, I recognized scoring opportunities by knowing I did something right or wrong. Then I would ask myself why I just did that. We all have a built-in right-or-wrong meter. A virtue or vice is always the underlying reason. Over time, it's easy to recognize them.

In the beginning, I set an alarm for every hour, to stop briefly and record a score: one point each time one of the V's was exhibited, good or bad. I think of the scoring system like the plus/minus statistic in ice hockey. As a player, you get a plus if you are on the ice when your team scores and a minus if on the ice when the opponent scores. I figure we are always on the ice, and it feels like the thin part most of the time. Obviously the virtues are the plusses, and the vices are minuses. I use tally marks, vertical lines like "IIII" for the first four, then a diagonal line for the fifth mark. At the end of each day, add up the totals of each. Then subtract the vices from the virtues. A net plus score is a win for the day.

After computing my score each day, I say a prayer of thanks to God for his help and guidance, then ask for forgiveness and help going forward. I end with a "Glory Be," since I once read that it is the best prayer to combat pride, giving all credit and glory to God. Compute averages for the week as well. Then set an improvement goal, and identify specific areas to work on in the upcoming week (more on that later). All of this takes very little time and is simple once it becomes a habit.

Here are a few other things for you to consider. Complete honesty in your scoring is essential. I suppose this should go without saying, given that honesty is a basic saint tenet. No one ever needs to see your score unless you choose to share it. The details are no one else's business. I try to score myself as I think God would. I try to envision myself sharing my score with him at the pearly gates with a straight face. I really don't want Him laughing at my self-assessment in front of all the real Saints.

In the beginning, stop to score yourself often throughout the day. The more you think about this, the more likely you are to choose virtue. You will become acutely aware of your behavior and the moments throughout every day when you make a choice. Some of those choices have become habits to such an extent that you don't even think of them as choices anymore. It's a very interesting and sometimes frustrating process. Striving for a net positive day was my first goal. Yeah, it took a while.

This simple game has quickly had an incredible transformative effect for me for at least two reasons. First, it helps keep my goal of sainthood at the top of my mind all day long. Second, I like to win, or don't like losing, so it provides constant motivation for me to be on my "A" game most of the time. I must admit that I was truly amazed at how quickly my attitude and behaviors changed. Instilling daily tracking as a habit took about three weeks. I was whining to myself late in the first week. I was losing and not happy with myself. Please commit to doing this daily for at least three weeks before passing judgment about whether you will continue.

Summary –

- Track your V behavior to become more aware of your choices.
- Develop a baseline score to guide future goal setting.
- Make keeping track a habit by committing to it for at least three weeks.

Action Items –

- Use the Flying V Tracker to keep score in the upcoming week.
- Add up totals and compute your net score daily.
- Compute your totals at the end of the week.
- Set a net score goal for the upcoming week.
- Identify and commit to one improvement opportunity for the upcoming week.

POSTSCRIPT

After using the FVT for a few weeks, I thought that something seemed a little off about the scoring. You probably noticed this too. Some of my behaviors seemed to have more impact than others, both positive and negative. It dawned on me that there were at least three types of behavior for which I was scoring points: my thoughts, words, and actions. I realized that my actions had a bigger impact than things I said. And things I said had a greater impact than things I thought. I changed my scoring to 3 points for actions, 2 for words, and 1 for thoughts. This made a big impact on overall results. Try it. I think it is more representative of our impact on the world, so I'm sticking with it. The same tracker and tally-mark system works.

Here is some really great news for you. It's a Catholic thing so I'm not sure how it works for the rest of you: Seek counsel from your spiritual adviser. (I'll bet some of you were wondering if I was forgetting something.) Every time you go to the Sacrament of Reconciliation (i.e., Confession), you get to multiply all your prior vice scores by zero, canceling your negative points entirely. Your sins are wiped away! I choose to believe the virtue points remain, but in any case you have a fresh start with the vices. How about that?!

I ceremoniously rip up all my past completed FVT's to remind myself that through God's grace I get to start over. This helps me not to dwell on the past, but to focus on doing better in the present. The world dwells on the past; we don't have to. I wonder how a priest would react to your handing him your completed tracking sheets to discuss the specific sins associated with your vice tallies. That could be interesting. You try it and let me know how it goes, and I'll be right behind you.☺

P.S. SUMMARY –

- Your thoughts, words, and actions have an escalating impact on the world.

- Your scoring should reflect this.
- The Sacrament of Reconciliation wipes away your sins and gives you a fresh start. Go often!

P.S. Action Items –

- Use the revised scoring system in the upcoming week.
- Establish a new baseline.
- Set a new weekly goal.

22

SAINTBALL

I T'S TIME FOR a quick recap of where we are on our journey to become saints. We have a shared Strategic Plan that contains the following:

- Vision – Revive heaven on earth.
- Purpose – Strive to become saints.
- Objectives – Love God and neighbors.
- Strategies – Do the right things the right way.

And a great beginning on our individual plans containing:

- Your unique Mission
- PLAYtime goals
- A PLAYground plan
- A Flying V baseline score and initial goal

You are using the PLAYtime Tracker, PLAYground Activity Plan, and Flying V Tracker daily in order to record your activity, review results, and plan your days and weeks. All we have left to do is expand upon this work in order to develop comprehensive plans to guide our lives in the pursuit of sainthood from here to eternity.

Nice work to this point! I trust that you are saintlier already. Got your halo yet? (We should design a "Got Halo?" T-shirt in the "Got Milk?" tradition.) I just did a search for halo to find out its origin and meaning, and all I got was a bunch of stuff about some seemingly violent video game. I had to add "saints" to the search to get this definition: "A halo is a symbol of holiness, represented by a circle or arc of light around the head of a saint or holy person. A halo can also be referred to as a nimbus." Got Nimbus?

What's next in our saint plan development? How about arriving at an overall grade on our performance? Let's make it a game and call it "Saintball." Not too original, I know, but I like that it rhymes with paintball. We are in a battle with demons, our own and those of this world, so the name seems appropriate.

The object of Saintball is to strive for sainthood. Recall that our formula to achieve this is RT x RW x G = S. Do the right things in the right way, then hope that through the grace of God we become saints. The right things are the PLAY categories. The right way is through living the virtues. We have been tracking our results in both of these areas. Let's use them to come up with an overall score and a corresponding grade.

I'm using a 100-point scale to compute a daily score and also a weekly average score. Let's allocate a maximum of 50 points to each of our major categories, the right things and the right way. Then we'll add them up and apply a letter grade to the total.

Recall that we each established an RT time-allocation goal, and we are tracking our results against that goal. Our primary RT goal is to ensure we are spending adequate time in the PLAY categories, those areas that directly contribute toward making progress on your mission. To get an RT score, I divide my daily actual PLAYtime hours by my PLAYtime goal. Multiply that result by the 50 total points available to get a score. For instance, yesterday I had 10 PLAYtime hours compared with my daily goal of 13. That's about 77 percent of my goal. Multiplied by 50, that gives me 38 RT saint points.

Arriving at a logical RW score was a little trickier. Here's where I landed. Use your net score from the Flying V Tracker. Find your score in the left-hand column of the table below, and give yourself the applicable points shown in the right-hand column. I arrived at this table based on tracking my results over several months. As we get better, it may need to be adjusted upward, but for now it seems to work. It's skewed to the positive, since I figure we deserve points just for actively trying. Plus, it's more motivating. I sure don't want us to get discouraged and give up too soon, or ever. One interesting thing I've learned: To score big RW points, you must have a proactive plan to demonstrate the virtues. Simply fighting off the vices will not work. Just a little helpful hint.

Flying V Net Score	RW Saint Points
>10	50
6 to 10	40
0 to 5	30
-1 to -5	20
-6 to -10	10
<-10	0

I actually eked out a net plus 1 yesterday. This score falls in the 0 to 5 range, earning 30 RW saint points. Combined with the 38 RT points, my total for the day is 68. Now for the final step, assigning a letter grade. Look up your score in the table below to find your grade. Oops, D! I hope my parents don't find out!

Total Saint Points	Letter Grade
91 to 100	A
81 to 90	B
71 to 80	C

61 to 70	D
51 to 60	E for Effort
50 and below	F for Fire?

I do a weekly review as well. Since I like math, I average my daily scores to arrive at a weekly score and grade. I quickly analyze my results to understand where I am succeeding and where I am falling short. And most important, I decide what I will do to improve next week. *Quit watching so much TV, Scott.* My everything-else time is twice what it is supposed to be. The ability to binge-watch TV series was invented by you know who. Back to work!

I've been tracking results in this way for a couple months now. My best, worst, and average scores to date are 73, 40, and 57, respectively. E-for-effort average. I could tell you exactly what I need to work on, but . . . nah.

Obviously, I've made a lot of assumptions in this scoring system, like doing the right things and doing them the right way are equally important. Regardless, I've found it to be a good overall indicator of how I'm doing, and it motivates me to strive to do better. Using the Saintball Scorecard (SBS), together with your weekly reports, you can very quickly assess your progress and understand how to improve.

It takes less than 5 minutes a day. Really, I just timed myself: 4 minutes, 33 seconds, to complete the PTT, FVT, PAT, and SBS, identify improvement opportunities, and plan for tomorrow. Maybe we can cut this time in half using the hopefully soon-to-be-developed app. Less than 2 minutes is my goal.

Did you know that in a soccer game the only person who knows when the game will end is the referee? He keeps the time on the field, and play continues until he blows the final whistle. Life is like this: Only God knows when it ends. All we can do is play to the whistle. This is why I recommend you do daily tracking. Live in the present. Do your best today. Plan to do better tomorrow. And keep on playing.

Print off all the reports at the beginning of each week, and fill them in at the end of each day. I find that just before bed, when all is quiet, is a good time for this. Calculate your saint points, and get your grade. Then look at the reports briefly. Celebrate your successes, and identify one thing you will do better tomorrow. Say your prayers and sleep well.

SUMMARY –

- You have come so far, so fast. Congratulations!
- Computing a daily score is instructional and motivational.
- Celebrate successes and plan improvements every day.

ACTION ITEMS –

- Print the PTT, PAT, FVT, and SBS at the beginning of each week.
- Complete each of them daily.
- Review results. Identify specific areas of success to celebrate and opportunities for improvement to work on.
- Review your schedule for tomorrow, and adjust it as needed.
- Say your prayers and sleep well, my friends.

PART 6

LIFE PLAN DEVELOPMENT

23

GOAL!

A SIGN IN OUR high school locker room read, "No Goals, No Glory." I think it was right next to the one that stated, "No Pain, No Gain." Since we are seeking the ultimate glory, we better set some worthy goals. And yes, there will probably be some pain involved in achieving them. Hopefully we'll get the gain and glory later. When I hear the word goal, I'm reminded of that soccer sportscaster who yells a prolonged "Goooaaalll!" with each score. Life is like a soccer match: up and down the field, rarely scoring, with only the referee knowing when the game is going to end. I really don't know much about the game, so give me an analogy break here. Back to goals.

If you want to accomplish big things in life, you must establish goals and make plans to achieve them. Goals are the results we desire to achieve; plans are the activities we perform to achieve them. As one of my favorite bosses always reminded us, "Please don't confuse activity with results." Results are what matter. Developing goals before plans helps to push us beyond what we know we can easily do and to achieve results that actually do matter. It's the "shoot for the stars and you may hit the moon" mentality.

If instead you begin by developing plans, you will talk yourself out of setting big-stretch goals. I emphasize this because as we go through this goal-setting process, you will be tempted to list all the things you want to do first and then to back into your goals. In fact, I'll bet you do exactly that in our first goal-setting exercise. Please resist that urge. Good luck.

At this point we know our mission, the right things to do, and the right way to go about doing them. All that's left is to actually do them. Simple, right? Should be, but life will get in the way. There will inevitably be distractions and temptations that throw us off course. Goals will help to steer you back on the right path. They will serve to motivate you when the going gets tough. To do so, they must be compelling and inspirational. I like this Andrew Carnegie quote, "If you want to be happy, set a goal that commands your thoughts, liberates your energy, and inspires your hopes." That type of goal will keep us on track.

Goal setting is another topic that has been written about ad nauseam. Amazon titles number 29,963 just today. It's lucky for you that I do have expertise in this field. I can summarize, simplify, and guide you through the process step by step. We are all naturally good at some things, and this is one of mine. Is this a time when it's okay to exhibit pride? It ain't bragging if it's true, right? I'll take the negative saint points if I have to.

Here's a brief overview of the balance of our saint-striving planning process. It builds on the work you have already done. You will have a complete saint-striving plan at the end of these next four chapters. Once complete, it will serve as your guide to doing the right things in the right way from here to eternity. Here are the five simple steps between us and heaven:

1. Develop saint-striving goals.
2. Develop plans to achieve the goals.

3. Take daily action in line with plans and goals.
4. Track progress.
5. Make ongoing adjustments as needed, and keep moving forward.

And add the step I always forget, Celebrate successes along the way. That's it, keep it simple.

We are each going to set a big life goal, as well as goals to be achieved in the next year that support its ultimate accomplishment. We will use the Goal Brainstorming worksheet in the Sandbox. The goals we will be setting will be designed to support accomplishment of our shared strategic plan and your individual mission. Those items appear at the top of the worksheet as a reminder. Write in your specific mission that you developed earlier.

The purpose of the big life goal is to make your mission more specific. This will help us to remain focused on what truly matters and to avoid the distraction of things that don't. In business I learned to set "Big Hairy Audacious Goals." This concept was introduced by James Collins and Jerry Porras in their 1994 book *Built to Last: Successful Habits of Visionary Companies*. The purpose was to challenge organizations to establish visionary goals that are strategic as well as emotionally compelling. We want to do the same, but let's call ours the Holy Spirit-Inspired Life Goal.

Here's your assignment. Find a quiet spot and give yourself about 15 uninterrupted minutes. Review the strategic plan statements and your mission for context. In prayer, ask God this question, "What do You want me to accomplish in this lifetime in order to fulfill my mission?" Sit quietly and write down whatever comes to mind without judgment. The words don't need to form a sentence; just write down the key words and thoughts that come your way. We will work on the more formal statement soon enough. Once done, continue your reading here.

Squirrel! As we approach the end of this process, my adversary keeps throwing annoying things my way. The cable company just ripped up my yard, a board split in our new hardwood floor, and our riding mower came back from the shop with a cut in the seat. The mower guys were great and are going to fix it with no arguments. The other two, not so much. I sure wish my patience virtue would overwhelm my wrath vice. (Just great, Scott, more minus points. Or as my daughter would scold, F minus! Got work to do there.)

Probably the most popular formula for goal setting is a system entitled SMART, an acronym for Specific, Measurable, Achievable, Relevant, and Time bound. It works. There are 489 Amazon titles to prove it. Is it really that hard to figure out from the associated words? I was just going to go with it but then noticed that the words smart and saint each have five letters. I wondered if we could come up with our own SAINT version of goal setting. Sure enough, it works, with a couple of minor changes. Here's my version:

- Specific – Easy for you and others to understand; what you want to accomplish
- Achievable – Challenging and difficult, yet possible
- Important – Worthwhile and inspirational; why achieving this goal matters to you
- Numeric – An objective measure of success
- Timed – Including a target completion date or timeframe

Here's a really good example of a well-written gigantic goal. President John F. Kennedy said this on May 25, 1961: "I believe this nation should commit itself, to achieving the goal, before this decade is out, of landing a man on the moon and returning him safely to the earth." Check it against the SMART or SAINT criteria, and you'll find that it meets them all. I looked this up to make sure I had the quote right. I found it interesting that the article stated that the goal was achieved on July 20, 1969, at 8:18 p.m. ET. I remember watching the landing and moon walk in living black and white. But the goal wasn't actually met until the astronauts were picked up safely in the Pacific Ocean on July 24. (Bet they would have had a hard time recruiting astronauts if the goal hadn't specifically stated the return safely part.)

Here's my goal as an example. My mission is to guide, motivate, and inspire people to strive to become saints. My goal is to inspire at least 3.5 million people to become passing-grade saints by 2025. "Passing-grade" means achieving 70 to 100 saint points consistently. We'll need our app up and running, and your agreement to let me see the overall combined results. It will all be anonymous and secure, of course. I chose 3.5 million, since it's about 1 percent of the current U.S. population. More math mumbo jumbo using geometric progression made that number appear doable by 2025. So there you have it. Seems crazy at this point, but so did the mission to the moon.

Take some time to write your Holy Spirit-Inspired Life Goal now. You can capture it on the Goal Brainstorming worksheet in the Sandbox. Have you ever heard the saying, "Perfect is the enemy of good"? Good is enough for now. We just want to get ourselves pointed in the right direction. Look at the SAINT goal criteria for help: Specific, Achievable, Important, Numeric, and Timed.

Warning: The next section may inflict some of that pain we need in order to get the gain. I've tried to make it as simple as possible, but it was even painful to write. Please try and stick with me. Have you ever water skied or tubed? When you are behind the boat, it's a nice smooth ride. Once outside the wake, it is rough and nothing but trouble. It's time for us to move outside the wake for a little while. I'll steer you back inside soon. Please don't ask my grandkids if I can be trusted on this promise.

We are now going to set goals for the next year. It helps to have goals that correspond with a calendar year because we typically have more time to think about them around the year-end holidays. If today happens to be near the end of a year, great. If not, think of the next twelve months as your goal-setting timeframe. You can revise these to calendar-year goals when that time rolls around if you so choose. Back to the worksheet. Take 15 to 30 minutes to think of all the things you'd like to achieve in the next year. Do this as a brainstorming activity, writing whatever enters your head with no judgment. No need to worry about the SAINT requirements yet. Go.

Now look over your list. Are any of the items activities rather than de-sired results? For instance, I wrote "exercise daily" and "eat less sugar." Those are things I want to do, but the goal is really to get to my ideal weight. Go through your list and label each item as either A for activity or R for result. Next, go through all the A's and make sure you have related R's for them. If not, create one. Strike through the A's once you have a related R for each of them, but make sure you can still read them, as they may come in handy later. Then, distribute the R's into the appropriate PLAY categories in the "Specific" column on the SAINT Goal Matrix in the Sandbox. You should have at least one goal in each PLAY category. If not, add one. More likely, you will have more than one goal in each category, which is absolutely fine.

The R's you have entered probably are not complete yet. That is, they don't meet the SAINT goal test. For instance, my R related to weight in the youthify category initially read, "lose weight." To make it SAINT-worthy, I expanded it to, "I will weigh 190 pounds or less by July 31, 2017." Does it meet the "SAINT" test? Specific, yes, if it meets the rest of the tests; Achievable, lose 30 pounds in three months, check; Important, I don't want to have to shop for new clothes, check; Numeric, 190 or less, check; Timed, July 31, 2017, check. Do the same test for each of your goals. Write them in a way that allows you to check all the SAINT boxes.

A few more things: It's really important that your goals give you a sense of excitement. When you visualize having achieved the desired results, you should have a feeling of great satisfaction. Anticipation of this sensation will keep you going in the tough moments, during the hardwork phase. For me, not having to shop is a strong motivation. (My wife would like to avoid that pain as well, the pain being me having to go to a store, ugh!) Achieving any worthwhile goal requires a strong commitment. To maximize your likelihood of success, it is helpful to create an intense sense of urgency, such as "I better get this done or else something really bad is going to happen," or "I don't want to end up with diabetes and all the life complications that go along with it." Take some time to find your personal motivators.

Here is a summary of other useful advice you will get from goal-setting experts. It is important to write down your goals. The physical act of writing makes them real, solidifies them in your mind, and signifies your commitment to them. Write them in a way that can be easily understood by others. Sharing with others further builds your commitment and enlists their support. Also, use positive statements in your goal. Notice I said, "I will" in my weight loss goal. There is no wiggle room there. It is more powerful than saying "I would like to" or some other less concrete statement. It allows for no excuses. Finally, post your goals someplace where you will see them often as a constant reminder.

Again, perfect is the enemy of good. I've seen perfectionistic types spend so much energy wordsmithing goals and plans that they never get much done. In business we called it the "Ready, Aim, Aim, Aim . . . (no Fire) strategy," as in "no fire in the belly" or sometimes, "you're fired."

When something gets a commonly understood name, you know it happens way too often.

Nice job on goals. Sorry it was a little difficult, and maybe time consuming. Of course, that is why most people never do it, but you are not most people! We'll get back behind the boat to smooth sailing soon enough. Now it is time to move on to planning how we will actually achieve these goals.

A goal without a plan is just a dream. Someone famous probably said that, and I hereby give credit to whoever it was. Wait, late breaking news, my Mom tells me that the quote is really, "A goal without a plan is just a wish," by Antoine de Saint-Exupery. I like it; he has "saint" in his name.

Anyway, setting goals without establishing plans to achieve them is like traveling without a map. GPS, you say? Well, wouldn't that be nice in life? We could call it a God-Positioning System. He tells us where to go and we follow. But alas, no such luck. Our path is unfortunately not made that clear. By taking the time to figure it out, we are practicing God's greatest commandment.

Oh, one last thing. We should all have a goal in our Act section that reads, "Become a consistent passing-grade saint (a monthly average of 70 to 100 saint points) by the end of this 12-month period." We can do it!

SUMMARY –

- No goals, no glory.
- Goals must be Specific, Achievable, Important, Numeric, and Timed (SAINT).
- Follow the process below to establish your goals for the next 12 months.

ACTION ITEMS -

- Use the Goal Brainstorming worksheet.
- Review our shared strategy.
- Write in your personal mission.
- Brainstorm your Holy Spirit-Inspired Life Goal.
- Write it in a SAINT statement.
- Brainstorm your desired results for the next 12 months.
- Review your list, and label items A for activity and R for result.
- Make sure you have an R for every important A.
- Strike through the A's so that they remain readable for future use.
- Label the R's with the applicable PLAY category.
- Write the R's on the SAINT Goal Matrix.
- Develop SAINT goal statements, at least one in each PLAY category.
- Include a Saintball grade goal in the Act section.
- Get safely back behind the boat, inside the wake.

24

PLAN!

THE GOAL CHAPTER title got an exclamation point, so why not the same for plan? They are equally important. They go together.

In my experience, most of us are much better at making plans than setting goals. Someone has probably researched this and discovered why. My guess is that it is simply more exciting. We get to do the things we plan relatively soon. Then we get to cross them off our list. It feels good to get things done. Seeing progress gives us a sense of accomplishment. Achieving a goal takes longer. It is the result of crossing off many activities. Oh, and most of us don't like that accountability thing. What if we fail? Sure, that's a possibility. But what if we succeed?! We have our goals, and we are good at planning. Name one decent reason why we won't succeed. I double-dog dare you. Let's make it happen!

Another worksheet? Yep, the PLAYground Activity Plan. Hey, I'm trying to make it easy. Three columns to fill in, simple. You already have one done. Write in your goals from the SAINT Goal Matrix. Remember, writing them helps with retention and commitment. You might as well write them again. Start with the first goal under Pray. Now list all the activities required to achieve the goal. Write down everything you can think of.

They don't need to be in order. Just brainstorm. I always put a time limit on my list creation. Five minutes per goal should be plenty. Take more time if the ideas are flowing. If not, don't waste time. You can always come back later. In the meantime, you are making progress. Progress is energizing.

Once you have a good list, add a timeframe for each activity. They may be daily, weekly, or monthly activities. That is, something you plan to do once a day, once a week, or once a month. For instance, under Pray, you may pray daily, attend mass weekly, and go to reconciliation monthly. Other activities may relate to a specific day, week, or month. Since we are planning for a twelve-month period, I usually use months in the beginning. If you had a goal to read the Bible this year, you could break that down into months first and then down to specific days. Search "Bible in a year" to find a plan you like; many have already been developed.

Here's my prayer plan as an example. I chose a goal of praying at least one hour every day. I want to make it a lifetime habit. I selected activities from the PLAY Plan Options Matrix. My plan is to pray every day, first thing every morning, last thing before bed, and the rosary at lunchtime. I will also attend weekly mass and monthly reconciliation. It's simple for now.

As with everything else, don't make this harder than it needs to be. Any plan is better than no plan. You will get better at this over time. Get started now and continuously improve. You are on your own to complete this. I've found that simple bullet points are enough. You know what you mean by them; no need to make it complicated. What's the enemy of the good? The PLAY Plan Options Matrix is a good reference source. Earlier, you also wrote your own lists in each area, which will be helpful. The Act section may take some time. If you are going to school and/or working, you probably already have plans in place, at least in your head. Review them in light of your mission, and see if they need adjusting. And write them down again.

Now you have your 12-month plan. Want to make it real? Have you been using the Playground Activity Tracker? Now that you have a more complete plan, you can use this form for weekly planning and tracking of everything you are doing. Transfer your routine activities to it. Those are the ones that you will do regularly, like pray every morning or floss every night. Also transfer any items you can do in the upcoming week. You can then use this form every day to make sure that you get all of these things done. Check them off at the end of each day.

One last step--I promise. At the beginning of every week, look at your plan and determine what things you can get done in the upcoming week. Put them on your plan and your schedule. This is called scheduling your priorities. Most people do the reverse: They prioritize their schedule. The activities you have on your plan are the most important things in your life. They were developed to help you achieve your God-given mission. Make sure they are priorities on your schedule, or they won't get done. Don't let this life slip away and get in the way of your eternal salvation. Don't allow life to happen to you. It is up to you to make your life happen and matter!

Check it out! You have successfully completed your plan to strive for sainthood. Congratulations! Find a way to celebrate. You will find that this is a huge step toward living the life God wants you to live. He and others will thank you. And you will be living purposefully for the rest of your days. Are you happy(ier)? The planning pain is over. On to the gain of taking action!

SUMMARY –

- Goals will not be achieved without a plan.
- Plans will not be achieved without scheduling your priorities.

Action Items –

- Complete the PLAYground Activity Plan.
- Complete the PLAYground Activity Tracker for the upcoming week.
- Make sure the planned activities for the week are priority items on your schedule.
- Take action every day!

25

REVIEW!

A NOTHER EXCLAMATION-POINT CHAPTER? Yep, still critically important. Now that we have our plans and goals nailed down, we need to take up our cross. Don't worry, this won't hurt. All that is left to do is to make it happen: Take action, carry out our plans, achieve our goals, and fulfill our mission--if only it were so easy. Inevitably there will be challenges to face and obstacles to overcome to remain on track. Never fear, a simple review process will help us keep the path clear.

You have already done all the hard work that will make this step quick and easy. It's a simple comparison of actual activity and results to plans and goals. Any large variations should be analyzed to see if a change in future plans is warranted. If so, revise them accordingly and move on. Notice I did not say a change in goals may be necessary. A change in plans is not unusual; changing goals should only be done if absolutely necessary, in fact, only when it becomes obvious that the goal is unattainable due to unforeseen circumstances. If you slip into a habit of easily changing goals, you will cease taking them seriously and all will be lost.

Allow me to introduce you to another important business concept: continuous planning. W. Edwards Deming, known as the father of continuous improvement, is credited with helping save Japan's economy in the 1950s. He is from my mother's birthplace, Sioux City, Iowa. Unfortunately, no one in his own country would listen to him until his success in Japan. (Bet the U.S. auto industry regrets that. What's the Bible verse about a prophet not being honored in his own land?) He taught many simple concepts and tools, one of which is that it is important to recognize that plans are not usually static, that they evolve over time. That seems obvious, right? Well, apparently not at the time. Anyway, he touted a continuous planning cycle he called PDCA (Plan-Do-Check-Act). Plan what you are going to do, Do it, Check how it's going, and Act accordingly. This simple process is used in businesses the world over now.

Small squirrel here. It always amazed me how often in business we insisted on making simple things complex. Looking back, I see that it is all pride-based. We get lofty degrees at schools where we learn fancy, complex stuff that we want to use. Or better yet, we develop something new that we can call our own and use to justify a promotion. We want to do it our way, not someone else's. I'll bet I've seen at least a hundred variations of PDCA. I even had to create one myself to make a sale to folks who wanted something innovative. I "innovated" PDCA into TAP, as in tap your potential. You will see how "brilliant" that is soon. So much wasted time.

If this process seems familiar to you, it's because you have already been using it. You developed playtime plans and goals and have been using the PAT, PTT, and FVT to track your time and activities. You review progress daily, make adjustments as needed, and plan for the next day. You are already completing the PDCA cycle.

Now that we have our full plan completed, let's discuss the Check and Act components a little further. To me, these are the glue that holds the entire planning process together, the keys to maintaining focus and driving progress. Think of it as flying a plane. You need to keep your eye on the instruments in order to know you are headed in the right direction. If you veer off course, you make corrections. Without these steps, you are flying blind.

Here are the simple steps I go through at least once a day. I run through them every time I have a decision to make as well. You guessed it, the innovative TAP methodology. Only three letters so it's obviously a 25 percent improvement over PDCA. I must admit that the TAP version I'm about to share with you is a little different than the business version I had created. You will see why in a moment. The steps are Think, Act, and Pray. You guessed it, pray wasn't in the business version. Pray is really the first step, but TAP is a better acronym than PTA. (I'd rather tap my potential than have the song "Harper Valley PTA" running through my head.) Regardless, it's a cycle, so "think" always follows "pray" anyway. Let's start with Pray.

Figure 25a   **TAP Your Potential Cycle**

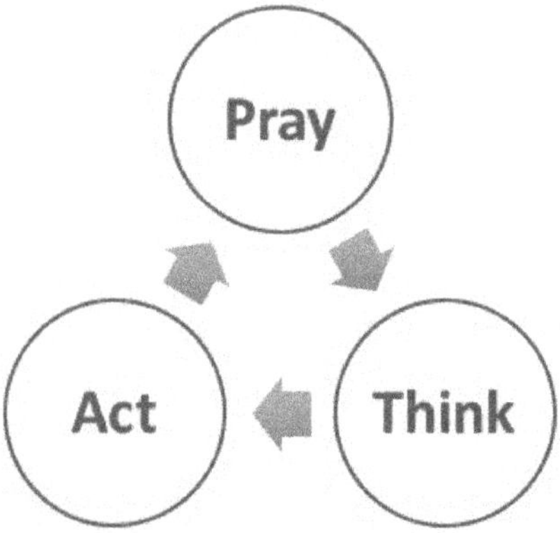

PRAY

Have you been keeping up with the Quick Start prayer suggestion? I graduated from the dummies ACTS prayer formula and now start my day using "The Prayer Process," developed by Matthew Kelly at The Dynamic Catholic Institute. There are seven steps: gratitude, awareness, significant moments, peace, freedom, others, and ending with the Our Father. Visit their site at www.DynamicCatholic.com for more details.

I now end each day with a process called The Daily Examen, developed by Saint Ignatius of Loyola. It has five steps:

1. Ask God for light – look at your day through God's eyes, not merely your own.
2. Give thanks – express your gratefulness for the day.
3. Review the day – reflect on your day guided by the Holy Spirit.
4. Face your shortcomings – identify them and ask for forgiveness and direction.
5. Look toward the day to come – ask for guidance for tomorrow.

Finally, throughout each day, I say a quick prayer every time I have a decision to make--a choice. Our lives are the sum total of our choices. Therefore, it seems prudent to ask for God's advice in those moments. Some of them will actually be moments of truth, those big decisions that truly shape our lives. Simply ask for guidance, "God, what would You like me to do?" Then sit quietly and listen openly. Your answer may come immediately or it may take time, but it will come. You might find this funny. Initially I was asking, "God, what would You do?" He once responded, "I wouldn't have gotten into this mess in the first place." I laughed out loud in church and decided to change my question.

THINK

Now think. Truly think about what you hear. Take the time. Make the time. People ask me what I like best about retirement. My answer: actually having time to think. The fast-paced business world never really allowed for deep thinking. There was always pressure to make quick decisions. Deep thinking was slow thinking and viewed as a weakness. I was once told, "We get paid to solve problems, not to think about solving problems." Interesting, think about that.

If you have patience and truly listen, you will get flooded with ideas, advice, guidance, solutions, and other helpful thoughts through prayer. Write them down immediately. Some will come quickly and others over time. The point here is to slow down your life to take time to think through choices. Start simply, using an "if-then" thought process. If I do this, then what will likely happen? If I make this choice, then what consequence will follow? Think through options as far as you reasonably can. Play them forward like you are playing chess; think at least a couple moves ahead or suffer the unplanned consequences. (Just checked Google, and there are over 45,000 book titles about thinking. I'm sticking to if-then for a while. Maybe add pros and cons later.)

ACT

You've prayed and thought, now it's time to actually do something. Take small steps daily that will lead to big accomplishments over time. Fifteen years ago, I got the thought through prayer that I should write a book about helping people become the best they can be. Guess the first step should have been to actually write something. Seems ridiculous that it's taken so long, but doubt and fear are powerful enemies to actually doing something. My if-then always had me homeless in the end. But I was not thinking from a God perspective at that time. Oh, me of little faith.

That's it, tap into our potential every day through the ongoing cycle of Pray, Think, and Act. Always keep in mind your purpose of striving to become a saint by spreading your joy through serving Jesus, others, and you, in that order. Tap your joy. Do we have too many acronyms to remember? Sorry, I came from an industry where every sentence you spoke was riddled with them.

Here's what I do every day before punching out. (Do timecard punch clocks still exist?) I complete the PAT, PTT, FVT, and Saintball Scorecard to get my daily grade. I pray The Daily Examen. Then I think about these questions.

- What should I keep doing?
- What should I stop doing?
- What should I do differently?
- What should I start doing?

Write down everything that comes to mind in each category. Yes, there is a worksheet for it. The "What Should I" journal. I use the same one every day for a week. It's very helpful to review in planning for the week to follow.

Finally act. Make plan and schedule changes needed for the next day based on your review. Relax and sleep well, my friends.

I use this same process every day. I also use it before the start of each new week, month, and year. Start with every day, and you will build a habit that will ensure your success for a lifetime. It will only take you a few minutes each day. You can spare them. Those minutes will save you countless hours, days, weeks, months, and maybe years going forward.

Are we done yet? I'm not, but you are certainly ready to roll. Put everything you have learned into practice immediately. I do have more advice, but most of it is motivational and inspirational in nature. Come back when you need some. And thank you for making it this far. I hope you are feeling as good as I am about making a positive difference in the world. And I trust you are happier than when you started. Those around you probably are too. Has anyone yet asked you, "What's up with you?" How did you respond? You should have a response ready. I just say,

"Keeping busy saving the world." If they ask me how, I tell them, "one person at a time starting with me. You want in?" Usually we laugh and move on. Try it. In the future maybe I'll hand them a book.

Summary –

- Review your progress on a daily basis.
- Use the TAP process to stay on track and make thoughtful choices.

Action Items –

- Complete the PTT, PAT, FVT and SBS daily.
- Pray The Daily Examen prayer to review your day.
- Complete the "What Should I" journal.
- Review your plan for the next day, and make any needed adjustments.
- Relax.

26

COMMIT!

THIS IS THE last chapter title with an exclamation point! Maybe it should have two or three. Making a commitment to your plan might be the most important step there is. Without it, nothing will get done. With it, nothing can stop you. Since you have made it this far, you are obviously serious about striving for sainthood. I'm truly impressed! You have been committed to and have completed 30 days of challenging work: the spiritual and intellectual effort of designing your future, deciding specifically what you are going to do and how you are going to do it. Most people have never done this. The ones who do usually succeed. They always do when they take this next step and truly commit to the sustained action needed to achieve their goals and ultimately their mission. They live their dream.

The reason this step is critically important to your success is that you will face difficulty in your quest. The first time someone questions your motives or something becomes hard to do, you might be tempted to give up. At the least, you will question your mission, asking "Is this really what I am supposed to do?" Probably many times. The closer I come to completing this book, the more this question is on my mind. I think my opponent is very unhappy I've made it this far. He is trying his best to erode my enthusiasm and get me to quit. He wakes me up often with thoughts of all that must be done to get this book published and marketed. Not to mention all the work that will follow in order to support all of you and to grow our community of wanna-be saints. Without commitment, I would have stopped by now.

To commit, we must ask ourselves why we are committing to this quest and whether we have the discipline it will require. Most things we do now because we want something--the me-first attitude, the what's-in-it-for-me mindset. Obviously saints are not me-first-type people. If your "why" is primarily driven by your desire to get to heaven, you will likely struggle. Rather, your "why" needs to be driven by a true desire to serve God through serving others. Can you create a compelling case for yourself around this line of thinking? At the very least, can you develop one over time?

I must admit to being selfish. I make all sorts of excuses for why the things I do are not selfish, but I know differently. I do think first, What's in it for me? Thankfully I've instinctively known that the best way to get what I want is to benefit others in some way, in other words, to provide value to get value in return. This mindset is what drove my business success, but the first thought is always self. I've been consciously working to change this for over a year now. Writing this has completely changed my attitude. I just visited my parents to tell them that I was working on this. Near the end of our talk, my mother asked what I was expecting to get out of this financially. I had honestly never thought about it. How about that! My eventual response was to maybe cover the costs of publishing and follow-up support work over time.

My compelling "why" is that I'm unhappy with the current state of our culture, as I mentioned in my old-man-rant earlier. I can keep complaining or do something about it. I can be part of the problem by remaining silent or part of the solution by speaking out. I can become a cranky, bitter old man who becomes increasingly ignored or help revive heaven on earth. The latter sounds much better, although I have always aspired to be the old man in the movie, *On Golden Pond.*

What is your compelling "why"? Will it be the other-focused "why" that will inspire and motivate you every day? You must find one. Time to ask for guidance in prayer again. Is that becoming a habit yet? As with all of my suggestions, keep it simple, don't try too hard, and don't spend a lot of time agonizing about it. Just start in prayer, then listen. (I recall something in the Bible about asking, seeking, and knocking.) I find that my answers usually come at some unexpected time. I make sure to always have pen and paper or my phone handy, with all that fancy stuff that I rarely use. The middle of the night is a popular time to get answers or ideas. Keep a notebook and pen by the bed to capture them immediately. Otherwise, you will forget by the morning. Write in big letters so you have some chance of deciphering it in the morning; trust me on that.

At this point you need to commit, delay, or bail. I hate when people tell me I need to do something; guess I'm still a kid a heart. Aren't we all? But in this case you really do need to make a choice. I doubt that any of you will bail, having come this far. But if you do, please hand this book off to someone else. You never know--they may succeed and bring you back sometime. Either way, you are potentially helping someone else who can vouch for you later. If you choose delay, giving the book to someone else may again be the best solution. Let's face it, if we delay, we probably won't get back to it for a long time. You might as well help someone else who is ready.

As mentioned earlier, my goal is to get 1 percent of the people in the U.S. to join our cause, 3.5 million. That many people spread out across the nation would certainly make a positive impact. We hear a lot of talk about the 1 percenters, those earning or controlling a certain amount of wealth. A quick search gave me too many definitions. The most interesting was that some motorcycle clubs can be distinguished by the "1%" patch they wear. This is said to refer to a comment by the American Motorcyclist Association that 99% of motorcyclists are law-abiding citizens, implying the last 1 percent are outlaws. As a silent protest of that statement many of the 99% wear the 1% patch for fun. How about we build a 1% spiritual community together? (Wonder what kind of overlap we will get with the wealthy and motorcyclists. Scripture says something about a camel and the eye of a needle, I believe. But then again, we all have the same purpose in God's eyes. We can all become saints. In fact, I have a wealthy motorcyclist friend who I have no doubt is in heaven. He died happy, riding that bike. Miss you, Chuck!)

If you choose to commit and have your compelling "why" to motivate and inspire you, congratulations! And thank you on behalf of God and neighbors! Your last commitment step is to print out your entire plan, sign, and date it. The Sandbox has a template for putting it all on one page with a signature block. Add a witness signature to further indicate your commitment, and have it notarized. I'm kidding, but you get the idea. You are signing a contract. Think of it as your covenant with God. You will do what you promise, and He will seriously consider providing His grace to complete our formula for entrance to heaven and eternal life.

SUMMARY –

- Make a serious commitment to carrying out your plan and achieving your goals.
- Know your compelling "why."
- Congratulations!

ACTION ITEMS –

- Put your plan on one page, use the Life Plan Template.
- Sign and date it.
- Have a witness do the same.
- Make it happen!

PART 7

INSPIRATION

27

SAINTSPIRATION

W HAT INSPIRES YOU? You have developed your saint plan and formally committed to it. You are highly motivated and taking all the right actions in the right way. You are excited and I'm excited for you too. Unfortunately, since I am a few steps ahead of you, I also know the excitement will wane at some point. For me, it took a couple weeks. I tell you this not to discourage you, but rather to make you aware. And as I think about that term, I realize that awareness is what this whole book is about: being aware of what we are doing and how we are doing it throughout every hour of every day. Otherwise, we go through life on autopilot, but without a destination or GPS. As a result, we crash and burn. Good news: There is a secret weapon to use when your motivation fades. I call it saintspiration.

A quick aside here regarding the difference between motivation and inspiration: Motivation is having a reason to do something; you know you should do something and you want to. Inspiration is being so compelled to do something that you will in fact do it. In short, motivation is the want to, and inspiration is the will do. It's the difference between knowing and doing. Those are my working definitions anyway. I think they are important because I see plenty of knowing in the world, but significantly less doing--and even more saying than doing. I take that back. There is a lot of saying one thing and doing quite another; does that count? "Do as I say, not as I do" is a common and seemingly acceptable excuse for being a hypocrite. Interesting.

We are all motivated and inspired right now. Making sure we actually stay that way is my desire for us all. I will feel that I have failed you if you ever quit. This is a lifelong battle for us all. I say "battle" because we are fighting a culture that makes it difficult for us to stay the course. I wonder how many times Jesus in his human form wanted to give up the fight. He was fighting every day. He fought using the virtues of course, but fight he did. He sure didn't choose the go-along-to-get-along path. He walked his talk and pointed out the hypocrisy all around him. I assume he had freewill, just like us. At the end he was exhausted, even sweating blood and asking for the cup to be taken away. Yet he sustained his faith and duty in the darkest hour. He persevered and fulfilled his mission to save us all. My hope is that we can too, with a little saintspiration.

So back to the question, what inspires you? For me the best source of inspiration is the example of others who have already succeeded. Seeing is believing. Once we know something can be done, it makes us confident that we can do it too. Learning what others did and how they did it is incredibly inspiring for me. So my first thought was to study the example of the big-"S" Saints. However, I learned two things quickly: (a) Many of them were far from saintly at some point in their lives, and (b) their eventually unshakable devotion and actions were extraordinary. Makes sense, Saints are anything but ordinary.

I really don't have the words to describe what I learned. I do have a word for how I felt: depressed. Even to become a little-"s" saint seems way out of reach again. Not a great way to end this book. Where's the high note?! I'm back to Ain't Me! My conclusion: Let's look to some everyday saint types for inspiration instead. Some of you may get the inspiration you need from the big S's. Give it a try and find out. Their stories are fascinating, but personally I find their examples so out of reach that giving up is a more likely outcome for me than trying to emulate them. Thanks, Mr. Glass-Half-Empty. I will continue to pray to them for strength and intercession, as they have my upmost admiration and respect.

Of course the trouble with finding the little-"s" saints is that they hide themselves. Humility is a great virtue to directly combat the greatest vice of them all, pride. But it also makes it difficult to spot those who can help us through their example. It's not like they advertise. We have to seek them out. And even when we find them, they will likely deny they have anything to offer. Is it possible to be too humble? My hope is that they will share their secrets with us once we identify them.

Currently this whole saintspiration thing is just an idea in my head. I thought about trying to identify those who have gone before us to use as examples, but I changed my mind. I would rather spend time finding living examples, people we can talk to and learn from firsthand. So how do we do that? We all probably know at least one person who is on the path to sainthood. Let's start there. What if we all just identified one? We could capture their stories and publish them for all of us to learn from. What kind of inspiration would we have then? Maybe we could get each one of them to nominate someone else. (Do they tend to travel in saint packs?) What if we found at least one in each Christian church in the United States? It is estimated that there are about 350,000 such churches in the country. Let's say there is already one likely-to-be saint in each. They could inspire two more each, and those two could do the same, and so on. You get the picture--geometric progression. We could get to 3.5 million aspiring saints relatively quickly.

How much change could we drive in the culture with that many striving saints? Who knows, maybe we are already there. If there are ten presently in each church we are already at 3.5 million. We obviously need more. I'm sure if we do our part, God will do His part and get those people to places of high influence. A quick realization: I bet at least one of you is thinking, Well, none of this is possible without God; there is no "His part" and "our part," it's all His. Understood. But we do have that pesky freewill, so I'm sticking with my description for now.

I'm on a mission to find those living everyday saints-in-waiting. Let's find them together. Here's my belief: Everyone has a story, and we can all learn from each other's stories. The benefit of telling our story is that we gain an awareness and a greater understanding of how we got to our present state. We can learn from it, plot our desired future, and develop a plan to get from here to there.

Our missions are interconnected for a purpose that only God knows. He expects us to work together. Recall that the greatest commandments are loving God and neighbors. What better way to show this than pursuing our purpose and helping others do the same? Wouldn't it be cool to have a Facebook-like site for aspiring saints? Of course the content would be a little different. We'd be helping to guide, motivate, and inspire each other. Maybe we can make a Saintbook together.

My pledge to you is that I will work to provide regular inspiration to help keep us all going—real-life examples, recommendations and tips, and a forum for sharing with each other. I'll certainly share what is and is not working for me. My hope is that you all will too. Feel free to join the conversation at saintbuilder.com.

You are saintspirational in some way--if not now, at some point in the near future. It's time to write your story.

28

YOUR STORY

W HAT IS YOUR saintspirational story? We all have one, and it is at least inspirational. We can add the saint part later. We may not realize it, but to someone our story can make a difference. I think it is important to tell our story in our own words. Seriously, who knows you better than you? It would be a shame not to pass along our unique experiences and learnings. We can all be teachers and students of each other. How many times have you said to yourself or others, "if only I had known then what I know now, I would have . . ." Why not help others with your accumulated wisdom and advice right now?

I'm at the age now when people I know are dying. I don't like it! I find it so sad when going to funerals that a person's entire life is summed up in just a few minutes. Three to six minutes is the recommended eulogy timeframe in case you're ever asked to give one. It seems like the same talking points apply to everyone. I always want to know more. Everyone should be required to write their autobiography at age 50. If you do, you are exempted from paying taxes that year. Same deal if you update it once every ten years thereafter. Good idea? I'd rather read your personal account than your obituary--your story in your own words rather than your eulogy in someone else's. Your U-logy. People think about leaving a legacy in their later years. How about we start writing and living our legacy right here and right now?

Earlier I shared some of my story with you. I had never really thought much about my story until that time. As I did, it helped to clarify my beliefs and solidify my mission. Taking the time to assess your life will do the same for you. I not only wrote my story to date, but also that of my future. That future version of myself is so much better than the past. It inspires me to keep pressing forward knowing that it is actually attainable. I recommend you do the same.

We rarely take time to reflect on our own life. You have now developed a plan for your future. Let's document your path to date, and add to it as you progress on your journey toward sainthood. Eventually it will be a saintspirational story that will serve to inspire others. You want to help others, don't you?! It's up to you to tell it. After all, no one knows it better than you.

In keeping with my promise of simplicity, I have developed a questionnaire to guide your thinking. Taking the time to complete it thoroughly will bring you clarity on who you are, what you believe, and who you will become. It will take some time and effort, but you will thank yourself for completing it. Others will thank you as well for what they will learn about you and from you. Basically what we will be doing is documenting the current state of you and envisioning the future you. In the meantime, keep working your plan. A common business saying is, "Plan the work and work the plan." Keep doing that. Feel free to take your time with this next step.

Step 1 is to get your box of "you stuff" out of storage. You know, that box or boxes of stuff you have been collecting since your youth. Check with your parents too. Boxes of photos, news clippings, yearbooks, videos, letters, memorabilia, etc. Step 2, complete the My Story Builder

Questionnaire in the Sandbox. Step 3, write your U-logy; the suggested format is also in the Sandbox.

It seems that in this age of fancy technology, there should be a simple way for you to answer questions, click a button, and have your story be magically written for you. Maybe in a future version; for now you get to write it yourself. It may take some time, but it won't be difficult and may even be fun. You will re-live some interesting times and likely find some pleasant surprises along the way. I did; check this out.

I discovered that I had personally witnessed Ernie Banks, Mr. Cub, hit his last home run. (I'm a lifelong Chicago Cubs baseball fan. The 2016 World Series champions . . . Finally!) Anyway, I found the scorecard I had completed for that game and noticed he had hit a homer. I wondered what number it was for him. Answer, number 512, his last. Cool, huh? I had no idea. I hope you find a neat surprise like that too.

A couple other interesting items: I got to play tennis with Rod Laver, considered by many to be the greatest of all time. I hit one past him and got a compliment on my backhand. On another occasion, my wife and I met NFL Hall of Famer and former Green Bay Packer star Reggie White and his spouse, Sara. I'm a lifelong Packer fan too. We got to spend a little time with them. When his spouse found out that we were Catholic, she laughed and said, "You people need to loosen up and have some fun." I replied, "We are too tired after the up-down standing, sitting, and kneeling workout." More laughter. Great people; rest in peace, Mr. White. We also met singer Tony Bennett. He was walking down the street alone in Salt Lake City, Utah. We passed by him at an intersection and one of our friends realized who it was. This friend whirled around and yelled, "Hey Mr. Bennett!" He waved us over and eventually invited us to come to the wedding he was singing at that night. We checked out the posh hotel, saw a few legitimate guests, and decided not to take a chance as wedding crashers.

One last recommendation before you get started: Read the following passage from an unknown author. In fact, read it now, read it before you write your U-logy, and read it again after. Then ask yourself, Will I matter? I have no doubt you already do and that your value to others will continue to increase through your ongoing work and example.

A Life That Matters – *AUTHOR UNKNOWN*

Ready or not, some day it will all come to an end.
There will be no more sunrises, no minutes, hours, days.
All the things you collected, whether treasured or forgotten, will pass to someone else.
Your wealth, fame, and temporal power will shrivel to irrelevance.
It will not matter what you owned or what you were owed.
Your grudges, resentments, frustrations, and jealousies will finally disappear.
So, too, your hopes, ambitions, plans, and to-do lists will expire.
The wins and losses that once seemed so important will fade away.
It won't matter where you came from, or on what side of the tracks you lived.
At the end, whether you were beautiful or brilliant, male or female, even your skin color won't matter.

So what will matter? How will the value of your days be measured?
What will matter is not what you bought, but what you built; not what you got, but what you gave.
What will matter is not your success, but your significance.
What will matter is not what you learned, but what you taught.
What will matter is every act of integrity, compassion, courage, or sacrifice that enriched, empowered, or encouraged others.
What will matter is not your competence, but your character.

What will matter is not how many people you knew, but how many will feel a lasting loss when you're gone.
What will matter is not your memories, but the memories that live in those who loved you.
Living a life that matters doesn't happen by accident.
It's not a matter of circumstance but of choice.
Choose to live a life that matters.

That's it, take your time and enjoy the process of thinking about you. It's okay for you to come first this time.

SUMMARY –

- You have an inspirational story.
- You are the best person to tell that story.
- Someday it will be a saintspirational story that will inspire others.

ACTION ITEMS –

- Complete the My Story Builder questionnaire.
- Write your U-logy.

29

GRATITUDE

H ERE IS SOMETHING that I think is really important, but that I have never done. I have thought about it for a long time but have never taken the time to make it happen. I will now and suggest you do the same.

In the development of your story to date, you were asked to identify those people who have had a significant, positive impact on your life. We should thank them. Let's send them all a personalized letter: an actual letter, handwritten or typed, sent to them through the postal service. It will mean a lot to them and to you as well. It may not be easy to find them all, but you owe it to yourself to try.

Start off by reminding them who you are and how you know each other. Tell them that you are writing to thank them for the impact they have had in your life. State specifically what that was, what they did, and what it taught you. Tell them what you have done and accomplished. Let them know early on that you are not on your deathbed, in case they were wondering. Tell them what you are planning to do. Thank them again. Send along a gift if you so choose. Give them your contact information. Let them know you don't expect a reply but that you just wanted them to know. These are just my thoughts. Do whatever you feel comfortable doing. I will also tell them I regret not having kept in touch with them. That is the case with many of my influencers, unfortunately. I really never thought about their impact until much later in life. I was just too busy to notice at the time. Poor excuse.

You may have a few "I'm sorry" letters you would like to write as well--maybe to an old friend that you had a falling out with or someone you wronged in school or elsewhere. You may have confessed these things through the Sacrament of Reconciliation to make them right with God, but it may be a good idea to make it right directly with these people as well. Of course, this is not required; it may be too painful. It may bring up too much of the past to be beneficial for the future of either of you. Leaving the past behind is usually a good strategy. Learn from it and move on. If making apologies helps you, then do it; if not, don't.

Look at your list of people to thank and prioritize it. It may take you years to get to them all, but make a commitment to do one a week or a month, whatever works for you. Just get started. You will feel better, and they will feel appreciated--a true win-win.

By the way, if you want to dive deeper into the world of gratitude, please read my Dad's book, *Gratitude, Affirming One Another Through Stories*, by Len Froyen. Yes, this is a shameless plug. Hey, he's my dad!

30

Conclusion

Y OU HAVE DONE it! You have a solid plan for striving to become a saint. To summarize, our shared strategic plan contains the following:

- Vision--Revive heaven on earth.
- Purpose--Strive to become saints.
- Objectives--Love God and love neighbors.
- Strategies--Do the right things the right way.

Our individual plans contain these components:

- Mission--Uniquely yours
- Goals--Designed to achieve the mission
- Plans--Annual, monthly, weekly, and daily plans that will serve to achieve the goals

You are striving to do the right things in the right way on a daily basis. You are reviewing your progress daily and making adjustments along the way. No doubt, you are continuously improving your results. What's your best Saintball score to date? Mine is 78, still only a C. Maybe that is a passing grade, or maybe it doesn't matter at all. John 3:16: **"For God so loved the world that he gave his only Son, that whoever believes in**

Him should not perish but have eternal life." Maybe grace is granted through faith alone. I still believe that demonstrating our faith through our works and behavior will be appreciated by God and neighbors. I'm going to keep striving.

My hope is that together we can create a movement, maybe even a revolution, with the aims of becoming the change we want to see in the world, of becoming the saints we were meant to be, of reviving heaven on this earth, and of populating heaven above at an escalating pace. I hope to meet you there someday. Let's all work together to save the world, one person at a time, starting with ourselves. We can do it!

I leave you for now with a prayer and a well-known quotation.

Serenity Prayer
--A version of a prayer attributed to Reinhold Niebuhr, an American Theologian

God, grant me the serenity to accept the things I cannot change,
Courage to change the things I can,
And wisdom to know the difference.

Living one day at a time,
Enjoying one moment at a time,
Accepting hardship as a pathway to peace,
Taking, as Jesus did,
This sinful world as it is,
Not as I would have it,
Trusting that You will make all things right,
If I surrender to Your will,
So that I may be reasonably happy in this life,
And supremely happy with You forever in the next.
Amen.

This following passage, commonly misattributed to Nelson Mandela's 1994 inaugural address, is actually from the book A Return To Love *(1992), by Marianne Williamson.*

> Our deepest fear is not that we are inadequate.
> Our deepest fear is that we are powerful beyond measure.
> It is our light, not our darkness that most frightens us.
> We ask ourselves, who am I to be brilliant, gorgeous, talented, fabulous?
> Actually, who are you *not* to be?
> You are a child of God.
> Your playing small does not serve the world.
> There is nothing enlightened about shrinking so that other people won't feel insecure around you.
> We are all meant to shine, as children do.
> We were born to make manifest the glory of God that is within us.
> It's not just in some of us; it's in everyone.
> And as we let our own light shine, we unconsciously give other people permission to do the same.
> As we are liberated from our own fear, our presence automatically liberates others.

Let's work to liberate one another to strive to become the saints we are all meant to be. Together we can make it happen. May God be with you all!

Saint Builder Sandbox

All forms including completed examples can be found at saintbuilder.com

Sandbox Index

A. Suggested Timeline

Week	Area of Focus	Chapters
1 (Days 1-6)	Part 1 – Introduction Part 2 – Strategy	1-5 6-8
2 (Days 7-12)	Part 3 - Mission Development	9-11
3 (Days 13-18)	Part 4 - The Right Things	12-16
4 (Days 19-24)	Part 5 - The Right Way	17-22
5 (Days 25-30)	Part 6 - Life Plan Development	23-26
At your own pace	Part 7 - Inspiration	27-30

Please note that the schedule only includes 6 days per week as Sunday is a day of rest. Personally I find Sundays to be great reading days. It might help to preview the chapters for the upcoming week on Sunday, but please leave the work for later.

B. Life Philosophy

Personal FROYEN Philosophy

- **Freedom** – *We all have the freedom to choose to do whatever we want (free will).*
- **Responsibility** – *With this freedom, comes great responsibility to understand the mission God has for us and to utilize the gifts He has given us in order to achieve our true potential.*
- **One** – *There is really only one person we can rely upon to make this happen.*
- **You** – *The choices we make and the actions we take all have consequences; choose wisely and act accordingly.*
- **Enjoy** – *If you are truly doing what you were meant to do, you will be happy. Adopt an attitude of gratitude for the opportunity to make a lasting positive difference in the world.*
- **Never** – *Never give up, and have faith that you will succeed by being persistent, patient, and confident that you will improve a little every day.*

General Life Philosophy

- *We all have a responsibility to recognize the potential we have to improve the world.*
- *We all need to hold ourselves accountable to realize that potential.*
- *It takes laser focus, hard work, determination and persistence, common sense, keeping things simple, and a constant striving for excellence to avoid the distractions that can interfere with our responsibility.*
- *Remember to incorporate fun into daily activities, be patient as difficulties are encountered, enjoy the process, be thankful, and celebrate the accomplishments along the way.*

Your Life Philosophy

_____
_____
_____
_____
_____
_____
_____
_____
_____
_____
_____
_____
_____
_____

C. Saint or Ain't Exercise

Instructions:
1. List the traits and behaviors that you envision as being saintly in the left-hand column.
2. Do the same for what you would regard as unsaintly in the right-hand column.
3. Answer the questions below.

Saint	Ain't

Circle the traits and behaviors in both columns that you most closely associate with yourself currently. Take a moment to think about the following questions, and any others you feel are relevant.
- Are they mostly in the saint column or in the ain't column?
- What are you doing well?
- In what specific areas could you do better?
- Do you truly want to do better?
- Are you going to be a saint or an ain't?

D. Mission Finder – Phase I

Current Mission (10 Minutes)
What do you spend the bulk of your time doing? _____
_____
_____

Who do you do it for? _____
What benefit do they get from it?_____
_____

Please circle your answer and explain. The word "it" refers to your current mission.
(40 minutes, 5 minutes per question)
Is it the best use of your natural gifts? Y or N
Why? _____
_____

Does it provide a significant benefit to others? Y or N
Why? _____
_____

Do you think about it and want to be doing it most of the time? Y or N
Why? _____
_____

Do you usually feel self-satisfied when you are doing it? Y or N
Why? _____
_____

Are you continually striving to become better at it? Y or N
Why? _____
_____

Can you see yourself doing it all your life? Y or N
Why? _____
_____

Does doing it encourage you to behave morally and are you able to do so? Y or N
Why? _____
_____

If you knew you were going to die in the next year, would you keep doing it? Y or N
Why? _____
_____

Revised or Alternative Mission (10 Minutes)
What do/will you do with the bulk of your time? _____
_____
_____

Who do/will you do it for? _____
What benefit do/will they get from it? _____
_____

E. Mission Finder – Phase II

Potential Mission (10 Minutes)

What will you do?_____

_____

Who will you do it for?_____

_____

What benefit will they get from it?_____

_____

Your Strengths (20 minutes)

What are your natural talents? _____

_____

What skills have you learned?_____

_____

What other strengths would you like to develop?_____

_____

_____

Your Interests (20 Minutes)

What interests do you have that could provide value to others? _____

_____

_____

What do others need or want that you could become interested in providing? _____

_____

_____

_____

Alternate Potential Mission (10 Minutes)

What will you do? _____

_____

Who will you do it for? _____

_____

What benefit will they get from it? _____

_____

F. Mission Finder – Phase III

SWOT (40 Minutes – 10 Minutes per box)

Strengths (Natural and acquired talents)	Opportunities (Needs or wants of others that I could fulfill)
Weaknesses (Traits to overcome or acknowledge)	**Threats** (Barriers to success posed by the world)

Potential Mission (20 Minutes)

What will you do? _____

_____

Who will you do it for? _____

_____

What benefit will they get from it? _____

_____

G. Happiness Index

Instructions:

- Fill in the years starting with your year of birth and ending with the current year.
- Complete the age column starting with zero in your year of birth. You may need additional sheets depending on your age.
- Rate each year using a 1 to 10 scale, where 10 is the happiest you can imagine being and 1 the unhappiest. Guess for the first few years☺
- When completed with your ratings, count the Number of Years corresponding to each rating grouping and enter them in the appropriate row. Add them all together and enter in the total row, That total should be one year more than your age if you have already had your birthday this year (if not it will be your age).
- Compute Percent of Total for each Score Range Number of Years grouping and enter in the corresponding row (divide the Number of Years by the Total and round to the nearest whole percent). The Percent of Total column should total 100 percent.

Year	Age	Rating (1–10)	Notes

Score Range	Number of Years	Percent of Total
8 – 10 (Very happy)		
4 – 7 (Neutral)		
1 – 3 (Very unhappy)		
Total		

H. Potential PLAY Activities

Pray

_____
_____
_____
_____
_____
_____
_____

Learn

_____
_____
_____
_____
_____
_____
_____

Act

_____
_____
_____
_____
_____
_____
_____

Youthify

_____
_____
_____
_____
_____
_____
_____

I. PLAYtime Tracker
Week of _____
(Record hours in boxes below)

Category	M	T	W	T	F	S	Total	Average*	Goal
Pray									
Learn									
Act									
Youthify									
Total PLAY									
Everything Else									
Total Awake									
Rest									
Total									

* Calculate the average by dividing the weekly total in each category by 6. Round up or down to the nearest half hour. The initial weekly average can be used as your daily baseline. Select a goal for each category based on how you would like to spend your time in the upcoming week.

J. PLAY Plan Options

	What	When	Where	How
Pray	• General • Standard prayers • Devotionals • Novenas • Daily Mass • Weekly Mass • Reconciliation • Adoration	• When wake up • Before bed • Before meals • Set times • Hourly • In big moments • Decision making • Help/Strength • Petition/Intention • Thank You	• Home • Church • Car • Work • School • Library • Anywhere	• ACTS Formula • Daily Examen • Kelly Prayer Process • Read • Memorize • Apps • Individually • Family • Group
Learn	• Bible study • Religion • School • Job/Career • Interests • Hobbies • Truth seeking	Schedule a standard daily time	Same as above	• Books • Classes • You Tube • Think for self • 10 ideas daily • Research • Create something • TV • Radio • Internet
Act	• School • Job • Home • Church • Volunteering • Networking	As scheduled	Determine based on specific activity	Determine based on specific activity
Youthify	• Exercise • Healthy diet • Drink water • Floss • Sunscreen • Hobbies • Sports • Games • Friendships	Schedule standard daily times	Determine based on specific activity	• Classes • Videos • Apps • Endless options • Find your fun • Add variety to keep it interesting

K. PLAYground Activity Tracker

Week of _____

Category	What	When	Where	How	Time	M	T	W	T	F	S
Pray											
Learn											
Act											
Youthify											

L. Flying V Tracker

Week of _____

Virtues	Definitions & Descriptors	M	T	W	T	F	S	Total
Humility	Modest opinion of one's own importance. Humble, respectful, servile, deferential.							
Charity	Voluntary giving of help to those in need. Alms-giving, benevolent, tolerant, compassionate.							
Kindness	The quality of being friendly, generous, and considerate. Friendly, generous, considerate, caring.							
Patience	The capacity to endure pain, difficulty, provocation, or annoyance with calmness. Tolerant, restrained, composed, indulgent, resolute, strong, serene, enduring.							
Chastity	The state or quality of being chaste; moral purity. Celibate, pure, innocent, abstinent, virtuous.							
Temperance	Self-restraint in action. Self-controlled, self-disciplined, abstinent, moderate.							
Diligence	Careful and persistent work or effort. Conscientious, dedicated, committed, tenacious.							
Total Virtues	Total of virtue scores.							

L. Flying V Tracker
Week of _____

Vices	Definitions & Descriptors	M	T	W	T	F	S	Total
Pride	An excessively high opinion of oneself. Vain, arrogant, conceited, smug, egotistical, considering oneself to be superior.							
Greed	Extreme greed for wealth or material gain. Greedy, covetous, materialistic.							
Envy	A feeling of discontent or resentment aroused by a desire for someone else's possessions, abilities, status, or situation. Jealous, covetous, resentful, bitter, discontented, begrudging.							
Wrath	Angry, violent, or stern indignation. Angry, furious, outraged, annoyed, irritated, irate, mad.							
Lust	An inordinate craving for the pleasures of the body. Intensely desirous, passionate, full of yearning, longing, lascivious.							
Gluttony	An inordinate desire to consume more than what one requires. Insatiable, voracious, rapacious, piggish.							
Sloth	Reluctance to work or make an effort. Lazy, idle, inactive, inert, sluggish, shiftless, apathetic, listless, lethargic.							
Total Vices	Total of vice scores.							
Net Score	Subtract total vices from total virtues.							

M. Saintball Scorecard

Week of _____

	PLAYtime			V's		Saintball	Score
	PLAY Hours	Goal Hours	Saint Points	Net Score	Saints Points	Total Saint Points	Letter Grade
Mon							
Tue							
Wed							
Thurs							
Fri							
Sat							
Total							
Average							

V Score Range	Saint Points		Saint Points Table	Letter Grade
> 10	50		91 to 100	A
6 to 10	40		81 to 90	B
0 to 5	30		71 to 80	C
-1 to -5	20		61 to 70	D
-6 to -10	10		51 to 60	E
< -10	0		50 or less	F

Instructions:
- Enter daily PLAY and Goal hours from the PLAYtime Tracker.
- Compute PLAYtime Saint Points by dividing PLAY hours by Goal hours and multiplying the result by 50.
- Enter daily V net score from the Flying V Tracker.
- Look-up the net score in the V Score Range Table and enter the cooresponding number of Saint Points.
- Add the PLAYtime Saint Points to the V Saint Points and enter in the Total Saint Points column for each day.
- Look-up the Total Saint Ponits in the Saint Points Table and enter the corresponding Letter Grade for each day.
- To compute Total Saint Points and a Letter Grade for the week, first compute an average for both PLAYtime and V points. The average is computed by totaling Saint Points for the week and dividing that total by 6. Round up to the nearest whole number. Total those points and look-up your grade.

N. Goal Brainstorming Worksheet
Year _____

Strategic Plan

Vision: Revive heaven on earth
Purpose: Strive to become a saint
Objectives: Love God and neighbors
Strategies: Do the right things in the right way

Your Mission:

_____

_____

What is your Holy Spirit-Inspired Life Goal?

_____

_____

_____

_____

Goals Brainstorm

_____

_____

_____

_____

_____

_____

_____

_____

_____

_____

_____

_____

_____

_____

_____

_____

_____

_____

_____

_____

_____

_____

_____

O. SAINT Goal Matrix
(Specific, Achievable, Important, Numeric, Timed)
Year _____

	S	A	I	N	T
Pray					
Learn					
Act					
Youthify					

P. PLAYground Activity Plan
Year _____

	Goal	Activities to Achieve	Timeframe
Pray			
Learn			
Act			
Youthify			

Q. What Should I Journal

What should I keep doing?

_____
_____
_____
_____
_____
_____

What should I stop doing?

_____
_____
_____
_____
_____

What should I do differently?

_____
_____
_____
_____
_____

What should I start doing?

_____
_____
_____
_____
_____

R. Life Plan Template

Name _____

Strategic Plan
Vision: Revive heaven on earth
Purpose: Strive to become a saint
Objectives: Love God and neighbors
Strategies: Do the right things in the right way

Your Mission:

_____

_____

Your Holy Spirit-Inspired Life Goal:

_____

_____

Annual Plan (12 Months) _____

	Goals	Activities to Achieve	Timeframe
Pray			
Learn			
Act			
Youthify			

Your signature _____ Date _____

Witness signature _____ Date _____

S. My Story Builder Questionnaire

Basics
Where were you born? _____
Where did you grow up? _____
What are the names of your close family members (parents, grandparents, siblings, other influential family)? _____
_____

Spouse name? _____
Children? _____
Children's spouses? _____
Grandchildren? _____
Where have you lived? _____
Where do you live now? _____

Journey to date
What schools have you attended? _____
What degrees and certifications do you have? _____
What are your main interests? _____
What were your childhood dreams? _____
Who have been the key Influencers in your life (family, friends, teachers, coaches, coworkers)?_____
_____

What jobs have you had? _____
_____

What do you do for a living now? _____

Moments of Truth
Plot your journey to date on the Happiness Index.
What have been your best decisions? _____
_____
_____

What have been your greatest accomplishments? _____
_____
_____
_____

What are your best memories? _____
_____
_____
_____
_____

Worst decisions? _____
_____

Lessons Learned
What have you done well? _____
_____
_____

What do wish you would have done differently? _____
_____
_____

What advice do you have for others (do's, don'ts, keys to success, etc.)? _____
_____
_____
_____
_____

Favorites
Books _____
_____

Quotes _____
_____

Songs _____
_____

Movies _____
_____

Sports/Teams _____
_____

Travel locations _____
_____

Bands _____
_____

Hobbies _____
_____

Stories _____
_____

Photos (Put together a collection)
Memorabilia (Note items and locations. Take photos)

Testimonial's
What would you like others to say about you?_____
_____
_____
_____

What do you think others would actually say about you? _____
_____
_____
_____

T. My U-logy Template

Introduction_____ chose to live a life that mattered. He/she loved God and neighbors, and spread his/her joy by always striving to do the right things in the right way. His/her mission in life was to _____. He/she did this honorably and humbly, never seeking any recognition. Seeing the positive difference he/she made in the lives of others was reward enough. I trust that _____ has been allowed entrance through the pearly gates and will live eternally in heaven as the saint he/she was on earth.

Specifics

_____ was born on _____ in _____

His/her parents were _____.

He/she was their _____ child. Siblings include_____

_____

He/she lived in the following places: _____

_____

School History _____

_____

Work History _____

_____

He/She met his/her spouse _____ at _____

and were married on _____ in _____.

They have _____ children, _____

and _____ grandchildren, _____.

He/she had many interests, including _____

_____

_____

and supported many organizations and causes, such as _____

_____.

He/she had many fond memories, including _____

_____

_____.

His/her favorite music, books, and movies were _____

_____

_____.

His/her advice for us all is _____

_____

_____.

He/she will be deeply missed for his/her always positive attitude, _____

_____.

He/she thanks you all for being a part of his/her earthly life and urges you to continue to live out your individual missions in the hope that through God's grace we might all live out eternity together.

ABOUT THE AUTHOR

Scott A. Froyen

A GRADUATE OF THE University of Northern Iowa, Scott started his career as a certified public accountant at KPMG, servicing clients in the financial services industries. He spent the bulk of his career in the health insurance industry as a leader in the areas of finance, operations, and sales. In all roles, he led development and execution of strategic and operational plans, continuous process improvement, and culture enhancement. His strong customer focus and desire to provide the highest possible value for the dollar earned him the unofficial title of fix-it guy.

He and his spouse Melanie met at a disco on a New Year's Eve and were married a year later on a leap-year day. They have two children, three grandchildren, and two dogs. He played collegiate tennis and has continued competing to this day. He also plays the drums in upbeat blues and classic rock cover bands and is a six-sigma black belt.

Scott has volunteered for many organizations over the years, his most significant contribution being as a board member and past chairman of LifeServe Blood Center in Des Moines, Iowa. He is also a member of the Knights of Columbus.

He recently founded The Saint Builder Foundation with a vision of reviving heaven on earth, and a mission of guiding, motivating, and inspiring people to strive to become saints. To learn more about how you can participate in this endeavor please visit saintbuilder.com.